ECONOMICS OF THE ROAD TRANSPORT

ECONOMICS OF THE ROAD TRANSPORT

RAVINDER N. BATTA

Publications

KALPAZ PUBLICATIONS

DELHI-110 052

Economics of the Road Transport

Rs. 690

ISBN : 81-7835-646-5

Published in 2008 in India by
Kalpaz Publications,
C-30, Satyawati Nagar,
Delhi-110 052
Email : kalpaz@hotmail.com
Phone: 9212729499

Lasertype Setting by: Tact Computer Graphics, Delhi
Printed at: Singal Print Media, Delhi

This study is dedicated to the memory of late Mr. Atma Ram Lamba for constantly motivating me to dive in this unfathomed ocean of knowledge.

Contents

List of Tables

List of Figure

Preface

Transport has a major impact on the lives of everyone. Even though the lack of transport in the developing countries acts as a serious drag on economic development, too much of transport in the developed world is the cause of serious gridlock, congestion, pollution and health damage. Traffic in the major cities of the world is seriously congested and results in loss of billions of dollars to the economies and serious disruption to everyday life (World Bank 1996). Further still, growth of demand for transport is a major factor in the growth of greenhouse gas (GHG) emissions and the problems associated with climate change. Local air pollution from transport in developing countries contributes to the premature deaths of over 500,000 people every year, and imposes an economic cost of up to 2 percent of gross domestic product (GDP) in many countries (World Bank 2002). It is argued that the gains from low emissions technology vehicles are offset due to increased kilometers of travel thereby pushing us further up the Green House Gas emission curve. From the Indian standpoint the most serious environmental impact is that of air pollution, particularly because of its effects on human health.

The intensity of the human health impacts from these emissions, however, is a function of the level of exposure. Many people in developing countries, because of lifestyle, economic condition, and occupation, spend large amounts of time in close proximity to road traffic and so are more exposed to harmful emissions. The problem is further aggravated by traffic congestion. Traffic congestion reduces travel speeds and in turn leads to environmental and economic problems because the traffic is congested with a mix of pedestrians and a wide variety of traffic modes. As a result, fuel consumption increases and so are the vehicle emissions, which further exacerbates air pollution and increases the noise levels.

However, the usual policy response to the problems of transport is to invest money in more infrastructure even though it encourages more traffic and switch over from public transport to personal modes. Unfortunately, these investments take a significant slice of the budget at a time when healthcare, pension and social infrastructure need more attention in the wake of rising costs and falling allocations in real terms. A suitable policy framework is required to provide incentive to the in-use obsolete technology vehicles to adopt new technology interventions. The road tax or the token tax needs to be so structured that the incidence of the tax reduces with the technological improvements and reduction in pollution emissions and increases with the level of pollution. Suitable tax concessions could be provided for four stroke engines in two and three wheelers, Euro-II engines in petrol and turbo engines in diesel vehicles.

While improvements in technology would certainly enhance performance parameters in pollution and road safety among new vehicles, attention also needs to be given to the in-use vehicles. Among the in-use vehicles, Inspection and Maintenance Program, Manufacturer Warranty Program and Scrape Program could help tackling the problem. One of the most commonly used methods of vehicle maintenance is the Inspection and Maintenance (I/M) requirement prescribed in Motor Vehicles Act. However, there are serious issues in effectiveness of such systems as they are mostly run on visual inspection basis without adequate mechanical support and are often amenable to gratification led short cuts. As optimal I/M systems are very costly, it is often recommended that limited resources should be applied to more robust test protocols to those vehicle categories which are likely to be gross polluters.

Extending the responsibility of performance to the manufacturer is also one of the often recommended options. Owing to the modest success of the current inspection and maintenance systems, there is a trend to shift the liability of maintaining emission control throughout the life of the vehicle on manufacturers through the warranty coverage requirements on emission control equipment. As the manufacturers would not like to be penalized through the warranty covered repairs, the quality of the equipment will improve. It is being currently achieved by making suitable provisions in the Central Motor Vehicle rules.

Modernizing the vehicle fleet by incentivising retirement is an effective option in this regard for India since the maximum life span of vehicles has not been prescribed. As new vehicles are cleaner than older ones, policies that encourage early scrap page of the older vehicles can yield significant emission reduction. One of the options used by many countries is introduction of a subsidy on scrapping a vehicle. The success of scrappage program in terms of cost effectiveness and emission reduction however depends on the amount of subsidy. If the subsidy offered is less than the selling price of the old vehicles, it may not be effective while raising the level of subsidy may reduce cost effectiveness. Besides, due caution has to be maintained to ensure that the subsidy does not reduce incentive to maintain the vehicle.

It is often argued (Litman 2003) that sustainability requires more efficient, equitable, and environmentally sensitive transport. Transport planners often treat vehicle movement as an end in itself. Sustainable transportation planning focuses on access, which can often be improved with strategies that reduce the need to travel altogether. Sustainable transport planning requires policies that reward individuals, agencies and communities for achieving sustainability objectives. There are many specific transportation strategies that can help support sustainability, including improved travel choices, efficient pricing, and land use. A third or more of current motor vehicle use could be reduced by eliminating market distortions that encourage inefficient travel. The transport policy has therefore to aim at this.

Development of alternate modes of transport to provide an efficient service for passenger and freight transport is also among the prime concerns of a transport policy. The emphasis is on development of environment friendly modes and non-motorized modes of transport. To improve the choice, comfort, convenience, frequency and safety of the road passenger transport, the vehicle design and technology has to be changed. Urban buses need air suspension, low floor and high carrying capacity and better seats for comfort, and should ideally be fitted with power steering to reduce the fatigue of the driver and thus reduce accidents. Another most neglected aspect is that of promotion of non-motorized transport system. In some developed countries efforts are being made to develop and popularize usage of cycling and walk trips by promoting pathways and cycling.

Transport sector could also contribute to poverty relief and promoting equity by improving the ability to access goods, services and employment opportunities. Externalities of transportation should be reduced by reducing pollution emissions and accident risks from motor vehicle use, or compensating those who bear the external costs. It also implies that the users pay for what they get which in turn implies more accurate road and parking fees and insurance pricing. Simultaneously access options should improve for people who are economically, socially and physically disadvantaged. It often means discounted prices for the disadvantaged.

A sound transport policy has therefore to address multiple concerns ranging from emissions, congestion, road safety, economic sustainability of the transport systems and meeting the requirements of the people and the industry to handling the sensitive issues like concerns for equity. Often equity concerns are neglected due to the reform led aversion among the policy makers for subsidization and cross subsidization. As the discussions in the book highlight, the problem could even be handled by rationalizing tax structures which are currently heavily loaded in favour of private vehicles at the cost of public transport ignoring the contribution of private vehicles to the adverse impacts of transport namely emission, congestion and road accidents.

This book is an attempt to highlight main issues involved in the transport management which often are ignored either due to the lack of information/ knowledge with the authorities or due to their over engagement with the regulatory work. I would like to thank the Institute of integrated Himalyan Studies and the Society of Indian Automobile Manufactures (SIAM) for funding this research/ publication.

Ravinder N. Batta
Shimla: 11-11-2007

1
INTRODUCTION

1.1 The Context

An efficient transportation network is a pre-requisite for sustained economic development. A good connectivity of habitations is often the primary means of supplementing the public effort directed at providing basic health and educational services as well as infrastructural support for production, trade and commerce. Efficient means of transportation and communication gain particular significance in the circumstances (as in India) where 70 percent of the population lives in the rural areas 50 percent of which are still not connected with road. Though the road transportation network has expanded manifold in the last fifty years of planned development, it, however, remains inadequate in terms of spread, is unable to handle high traffic density at many places and has poor riding quality in some segments (MORTH 2005). One of the major reasons for its inadequacy is rise in the transport demand much more than the road capacity during this period. Among the key factors that have affected the transport demand are increases in population, household incomes, industrial and commercial activities and leisure travel demand.

Within the transport sector, road transport generally constitutes a bigger segment. It is estimated that in India as against 5.5 percent GDP contributed by all means of transport, 3.69 percent comes from the road transport alone (MORTH 2005). Many factors contribute to the dominance of the road transport. First, is the location of enterprises. With production centers moving away from the urban centers to specific industrial zones, these industrial zones often lie outside the urban sphere of influence and lack adequate connections to railways and inland navigation. Second, there has been a strong evolution towards new production structures, whereby transport has been integrated into the production logistics of enterprises. The greater the value of the goods concerned, the more important speed and flexibility become in transportation. Finally, with the nature of goods produced changing overtime, there has been a reduction in transportation of bulk goods like raw material having high specific gravity and low value added. The trend towards the transportation of finished products with a high value added has benefited the road haulage sector.

The combined effect of these developments results in transport of lower volumes over larger distances, expressed in tonne-kilometres. This leads either to a rise or a decline, depending on the specific circumstances. Both trends favour road and air transport, since the time-related costs (capital costs of the transported goods) are becoming relatively more important. A major explaining factor for the growth in the road sector's market share can be found here: both the technical developments and the changes in relative importance of the different economic sectors have led to a considerable change in the value/weight ratio (Mayeres 2003).

World Bank (1996) takes this discussion a step further by exploring the reverse relationship: the impact of transport activities on economic development and growth. The argument proceeds like this. New roads lower costs of goods and services, facilitate the development of new areas, create new job opportunities and allow the development of urban areas where people and ideas meet and interact. Lack of transportation in the developing countries acts as a serious drag on economic development and a burden on women who carry water, fuel and crops over hundred of kilometers (Whitelegg 2003). Some stylized facts, obtained from World Bank (1996) are:

- Value added by transport is estimated to account for 3 to 5 percent of GDP.
- Public investment in transport typically accounts for between 2.0 and 2.5 percent of GDP and may rise as high as 3.5 percent in countries modernizing outdated transport infrastructure or building new transport infrastructure.
- Transport likewise commonly accounts for 5 to 8 percent of total paid employment;
- Demand for freight and passenger transport in most developing and transition countries is growing 1.5 to 2.0 times faster than GDP and the bulk of this increase is for road transport;

- Although demand for freight transport in industrialized countries grows less rapidly than GDP, in developing and transition countries the growth rate is closer to that of passenger transport.

Macroeconomic cross-country evidence shows that investment in the transport sector promotes growth by increasing returns to private investment. The estimated economic rate of return of projects in the transport sector is 22 percent, which is 50 percent higher than the World Bank average.

Even as the benefits from transport can never be overstated, there are a series of transport related costs that should be considered in assessing the relative advantages. Such costs are usually external to those who make use of transport and are often unaccounted for. When households and firms decide whether or not to travel, when and at what distance to travel and by which mode and route, they take into account only their own costs and benefits. Each additional transport user also generates costs to other transport users and to the society in general, which he does not or only partially takes into account in his decision process. The resulting traffic demand is too high in comparison with the social optimum, and is concentrated too much at particular times of day with share of the different modes being sub optimal. The costs that are not taken into account are external costs. The main external costs of transport use are congestion, accidents and environmental costs. These costs arise not only in monetary sense, but also in terms of time losses, accident costs, pollution, and noise.

The marginal external congestion costs are present whenever an additional vehicle in the transport network reduces the speed of the other transport users. A lower speed has several effects: it affects the operating costs of the other transport users, and their time costs that depend on the value of transport time. The fundamental defining relationship is speed–flow curve which shows that the more traffic on the road, the slower it goes, the effect becoming more and more severe as the traffic flow approaches the maximum capacity of the network. Congestion costs have become a matter of great concern in the developed economies while the developing economies are now trying to understand the true costs associated with congestion. It is estimated that congestion costs for the United Kingdom as a whole is about 20 billion pounds per year (Goodwin 2003). As congestion is a problem that cannot be totally eradicated, the literature on congestion cost has evolved from 'total cost of congestion' to 'economic value that can be saved with congestion charging' (Goodwin 2003). The emphasis now is on estimating the full economic benefits of congestion arising in the form of efficiency gains occurring due to improved access to labor and produce markets and increased pressure of competition over a wider area.

The marginal environmental costs, on the other hand, include the costs imposed by the emission of air pollutants and noise on society in general and on future generations (in the case of air pollution and global warming). The emission of suspended particulate matter (SPM) and sulphur dioxide (SO_2) by the motor vehicles causes damage to the human health. These effects include mortality (premature death) and morbidity (increase of chronic heart and lung disease. As per World Health Organisation estimates (WHO 2003) 4 to 8 percent deaths occur worldwide due to air pollution related problems. Some studies conducted in the USA (Mayeres 2003) have found that particulates have a statistically significant impact on morbidity also. Increased risk of morbidity results in direct economic costs related to efforts to reduce exposure, expenditure on medication and health care, lost earnings due to illness and reduction in welfare due to pain and suffering (Freeman 1985). The state of the art methodology for the quantification of the environmental costs is the Impact Pathway Approach (Friedrich and Bickel 2001). This approach proceeds in four steps. It first seeks to determine the emission caused due to an additional vehicle; then the resulting ambient concentrations are calculated; impact of these changes on health, crops, and materials are derived; and then finally the valuation of these impacts. Thus reducing vehicular pollution has significant health benefits. However, these cannot be achieved free of cost: abatement measures would entail costs. For example environmental taxes on gasoline or scrapping old vehicles leads to economic costs; phasing out leaded petrol requires investment in retrofitting the carburetor engine to fuel injection system; and changing over to CNG also imposes retrofitting costs.

The marginal external accident costs are not straightforward to define. When an additional vehicle joins the traffic flow, it causes three types of costs to the society (Mayeres 2003). First, the transport user himself is exposed to an accident risk. The social costs of this consist of his own utility loss due to the accident risk (which is internal), the pure economic costs associated with the accident risk (net output loss, medical costs, and police costs), and possibly also the utility loss of relatives and friends. Second, the additional transport user may have an impact on the accident risk of the other infrastructure users and therefore on the associated costs for society. Third, other transport users will adapt their behavior when confronted with a changed traffic situation. They can do so in many ways, for example, by installing safety equipment, by switching to safer modes by taking more care. Naturally therefore, risk avoidance entails costs that need to be accounted for. As the accidental risks are insured, the extent of externality in this case depends on the liability and compensation rules that are in effect, and on the type of insurance pricing. Any analysis in this regard will also need to take into account this factor.

These externalities are characterized by a feedback effect: the level of externality itself affects the behaviour of the economic agents. For example, congestion causes time costs which affect demand for passenger and freight traffic. Similarly, accident risks influence transport demand, modal choice, route selection and driving behaviour. Feedback effects can also be seen in air pollution and noise, since these lead to aversive or mitigating behaviour. As different externalities are interconnected, one externality may become the catalytic agent for another. For example, a reduction in speed will reduce pollution and accident risks. Since these are not perfectly correlated, different instruments are required to tackle them.

The government can make use of several instruments to tackle these problems. These are often classified into three broad headings (Mayeres 2003): pricing, regulation, and infrastructure policy related. These three instruments however, include a range of measures. For instance, pricing includes economic instruments such as fuel taxes, taxes on vehicle ownership, insurance pricing and road pricing. Regulation includes emission standards, speed limits, safety standards, and rationing of car use. Infrastructure policy includes measures to enhance the capacity of infrastructure and spatial planning. As one instrument does not preclude another, they are often used in combination with one another.

1.2 Sustainable Transportation

In the above background with transport activities impacting negatively, it is essential to factor in sustainable transportation in the transport planning and policy making. There has been a growing interest in sustainability, sustainable development and sustainable transport. While these have been in focus in recent research world wide, their implications for transportation planning and policy are only beginning to be explored (Litman and Burwell 2003). The goal of sustainable transportation is to ensure that environment, social and economic considerations are factored into decisions affecting transportation activity. Interest in sustainability originally started with reflection of concerns of depletion of natural resources specially the energy resources. However, later current equity and environmentally impacts of human actions also became focus of concern. Litman and Burwell (2003) explore the various dimensions of sustainability and the issues involved therein. Broadly, the concerns of sustainability can be arranged in three headings: economic, social and environmental. Figure-1 illustrates various sustainability issues.

Even though each issue may appear to be fitting into a specific category, in practice there is often an overlap. For example, on the face of it, pollution may appear to be an environmental concern, its impact on health and other economic

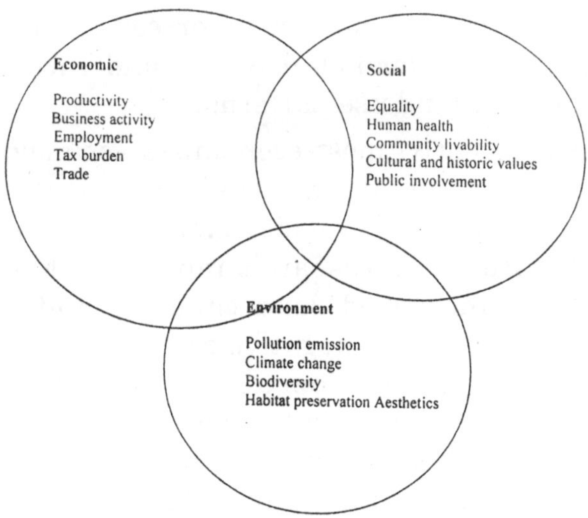

Figure 1: Sustainability Issues.

activities would stimulate economic and social concerns. It is therefore, paramount that the solutions to problems of sustainability reflect integrated analysis.

As transportation activities have sustainability related impacts, it is important to identify strategies that help achieve multiple objectives, and avoid those that solve one transportation problem and exacerbate others. For example, a policy or program that reduces traffic congestion but increases air pollution emissions or crashes cannot be considered a sustainable solution. Similarly, a strategy that reduces energy consumption and air pollution emission, but increases traffic congestion, crashes and consumer costs is not necessarily a sustainable strategy. The most sustainable strategies are those that simultaneously help reduce traffic congestion, pollution, crashes and consumer costs, increase mobility options for non-drivers, and encourages more efficient land use patterns.

Until recently, most economists assumed that whatever its social and environmental costs, increased transport provides significant economic benefits. But new research indicates (Mayeres 2003) that increased road capacity and motor vehicle use may have negative as well as positives economic impacts because the marginal productivity of increased transport are declining, and vehicle use imposes external costs that can offset direct economic gains. This implies that sustainability planning does not always require tradeoffs between economic, social and environmental objectives, but rather a matter of finding strategies that help achieve all of these objectives over the long-term by increasing transportation system efficiency.

Transport problems and solutions can be viewed in two different ways. One is as *individual problems with technical solutions*: traffic and parking congestion require building more roads and parking facilities; crash risk requires roads and vehicles that offer greater crash protection; energy problems require alternative fuels and efficiency standards; mobility for non-drivers in automobile-oriented areas requires para transit services. The motto is, "adjust roads and vehicles, not driver behavior". This approach is considered to have a fundamental flaw: solutions to one problem often exacerbate other, particularly if they increase total vehicle travel. For example, over the long run, increasing roadway capacity tends to increase overall vehicle travel by inducing vehicle use which increases crashes, energy consumption and pollution. Policies aimed at crash protection require heavier vehicles that consume more energy while the fuel efficiency standards reduce per-mile cost of driving further stimulating traffic congestion and crashes. Hence, this approach cannot solve all problems because the more a solution achieves its objectives, the more it exacerbates other problems.

The alternate perspective relies on market oriented analysis of transportation problems. It is believed that most transportation problems share a common root: *market distortions resulting in excessive automobile use*. From this perspective, solving transport problems requires planning reforms that increase transport options, and market reforms that give consumers suitable incentives to choose the best option for each individual trip. The motto is, "increase transportation system diversity and efficiency." Transportation Demand Management is the general term for this approach.

Transportation Demand Management (TDM) (also known as *Mobility Management*) is a general term for various strategies that increase transportation system efficiency. TDM treats mobility as a means to an end, rather than an end in itself. It helps meeting the transport needs in the most efficient way that reduces total vehicle traffic. The emphasis is on prioritizing travel based on the value and costs of each trip. Higher value and lower cost trips are given priority over lower value, higher cost travel. It increases overall system efficiency. Contrary to the general belief, the transport demand management strategies often emphasize on the movement of people and goods, rather than motor vehicles, and so gives priority to public transit, ridesharing and non motorized travel, particularly under congested urban conditions.

1.3 Road Transport in India

As per the motor vehicles statistics maintained by the Government of India, the annual rate of growth of motor vehicles in India was around 9.7 percent during the last decade (CIRT 2005). From 19177 million vehicles in 1990, the population increased to 58863 million in 2002. Traffic composition in India is of a mixed nature: there is a wide variety of both slow and fast moving vehicles.

The modal split indicates that in 1990 about 65.7 percent of total vehicles were two-wheelers, which increased to 70.1 percent within one decade. Percentage share of private vehicles (two wheelers and cars taken together) has also increased during 1990s (from 79.7 percent in 1990 to 82.6 percent in 2000). This is primarily because growth rate in two-wheeler population is higher than that of other vehicles (CIRT 2005).

Another discerning feature of vehicle population has been that between 1990 to 2000, two-wheeler and car (including jeeps and taxis) grew at a rate of 10.4 and 8.4 percents per year respectively, whereas the growth rate in bus population was 6.5 percent per annum. During the same period, goods vehicle grew at a rate of around 8 percent annum. Although total bus population in India is growing at modest rate of around 6.5 percent per annum, its growth in private sector is far greater than in the public sector. During 1990s, number of buses under the control of State Transport Undertakings (STUs) grew at a rate of around 1 percent per annum whereas private sector bus population grew at a rate of around 8.6 percent per annum. In the absence of an adequate and efficient public transport in India, a large number of private and para-transit modes have entered into the market to meet the travel demand. Such a proliferation of vehicles results in acute congestion, inordinate delays, serious accidents, high-energy consumption particularly of fossil fuels, and intense pollution of the environment.

The level of travel demand in India is increasing substantially over the years. Three factors contribute to this. The first is the increase in population. The second factor is the mobility rate, that is, average trips per person per day. Mobility rate in India is continuously increasing over the years. For example, in Delhi, average number of trips per person per day have increased from 0.49 percent during 1969 to 1.10 during 2001 (Table-1). The third factor contributing to travel demand is the increase in trip length due to increase in the physical expansion of the city and town.

Table 1.1 : Average number of trips per person per day in Delhi

Purpose	*1969*	*1981*	*2001(Estimated)*
Work	0.29	0.35	0.45
Education	0.08	0.10	0.15
Others	0.12	0.27	0.50
All purpose	0.49	0.72	1.10

Source : Ranganathan (1995).

A serious consequence of such a development is steep rise in demand for transport in almost all the cities in India. Tata Energy Research Institute (TERI), New Delhi, estimates this to increase from 335 Billion Passenger-Kilometers (BPKm) in 1991 to 1905 BPKm by 2001 for selected seventeen towns as per its study. RITES have estimated 462 million passengers trips per day (mptd) by 2016, for the class I cities (1,00,000 plus population) alone (CIRT 2005).

In terms of external effects, data on road accidents for selected countries given in Table-1.2 reveals that the number of fatalities per thousand vehicles is higher in developing countries like China and India as compared to developed countries.

Table 1.2 : Road accidents data for 2002

S.No.	Country	Persons killed (Nos.)	Population (10000 persons)	No. of vehicles (10000 vehicles)	Fatalities (per 10000 persons)	Fatalities (per10000 vehicles)
1.	Australia	1723	1964.1	1245	0.88	1.38
2.	Austria	956	803.3	533.8	1.19	1.79
3.	Belgium	1486	1026	573.7	1.45	2.59
4.	Canada	2779	3141	1810.2	0.88	1.53
5.	France	7655	5934	3540	1.29	2.16
6.	Germany	6842	8244	5330	0.83	1.28
7.	Japan	9575	12743	8097	0.75	1.18
8.	Sweden	532	890	493	0.59	1.08
9.	U.K	3581	5921	3040	0.60	1.18
10.	USA	42815	28837	22569	1.48	1.90
11.	China	106000	127000	6200	0.83	17.10
12.	India	82717	103700	5886	0.79	14.05

Source : CIRT (2005)

However, the nature of problem in developing countries is in many ways different from that in the industrialized world. The proportion of commercial and public service vehicles involved in road accidents are often much greater in India. Pedestrians and cyclists are often the most vulnerable. Most of the fatalities in the developed world are people inside the vehicle and therefore major efforts are made to make vehicles safer for the occupants. In India, since the majority of road users consist of pedestrians, cyclists and two wheeler riders, any transport policy has to address these vulnerable road users.

During the year 2002, 82,700 persons were killed and 4,04,800 were injured in total of 4,02,200 road accidents in India. Although fatality rate (defined as, number of fatalities per 10,000 vehicles) in India is declining over the years, it is still quite high in comparison to developed world. Road accidental deaths in cities are relatively higher than the Indian average.

On the pollution emissions also the situation is equally bad. Vehicular emissions depend on vehicle-km, vehicle speed, age of vehicle, and of course emission rate of different vehicle categories. Table-1.3 presents emission factors for different types of vehicles, under typical conditions, in Indian cities. One can see that emission rate, defined as quantity of pollutants emitted per vehicle-km, pertaining to carbon monoxide (CO) and hydrocarbons (HC) is very high for personalized modes (cars and two-wheelers) and para transit modes (three-wheelers) in comparison to buses, trucks, and LCVs. With deteriorating level of mass transport services and increasing use of personalized motor vehicles, vehicular emission is assuming serious dimensions in most of the Indian cities. The pollution load in major cities of India is given in Table-1.4.

Table 1.3: Emission rate of different vehicles in a typical Indian city (in gms/km)

Vehicle	*CO*	*HC*	*NOx*	*SO_2*	*Pb*	*PSP*
Two-wheeler	8.30	5.18	-	0.013	0.004	-
Car	24.03	3.57	1.57	0.053	0.012	-
Three-wheeler	12.25	7.77	-	0.029	0.009	-
Bus	4.38	1.33	8.28	1.441	-	0.275
Truck	3.43	1.33	6.48	1.127	-	0.450
LCV	1.30	0.50	2.50	0.400	-	0.100

Source: Sibal and Sachdeva (2001)

Table 1.4 : Estimated vehicular emission load in selected metropolitan cities in India

Name of the city Vehicular pollution load (tones per day)

Particulates	*Sulphur*	*Oxide of the Hydrocarbons*	*Carbon dioxide*	*Nitrogen*	*monoxide*
Delhi	12.77	8.96	110.45	184.37	421.84
Mumbai	5.59	4.03	70.82	108.21	189.55
Bangalore	2.62	1.76	26.22	78.51	195.36
Kolkata	3.25	3.65	54.69	43.88	188.24
Ahmedabad	2.95	2.89	40.00	67.75	179.14
Pune	2.39	1.28	16.20	73.20	162.24
Chennai	2.34	2.02	28.21	50.46	143.22
Hyderabad	1.94	1.56	16.84	56.33	126.17
Jaipur	1.18	1.25	15.29	20.99	51.28
Kanpur	1.06	1.08	13.37	22.24	48.42
Lucknow	1.14	0.95	9.68	22.50	49.22
Nagpur	0.55	0.41	5.10	16.32	34.99
Grand total	**35.31**	**29.84**	**422.88**	**809.96**	**2299.21**

Source : (CIRT 2005).

The average peak hour speed in Indian cities is far less than the optimum one. The quantity of all the three major air pollutants (namely, CO, hydrocarbons, and nitrogen oxides) drastically increases with reduction in motor vehicle speeds. For example, at a speed of 75 kmph, emission of CO is 6.4 gm/veh.-km, which increases by five times to 33.0 gm/veh.-km at a speed of 10 kmph. Similarly, emission of hydrocarbons, at the same speeds, increases by 4.8 times from 0.93 to 4.47 gm/veh.-km. thus, traffic congestion not only decreases the vehicle speed but also increase the pollution level (CIRT 2005).

1.4 Organisation of the Book

Chapter 2 of the book explores the micro-economic basis of Transport Economics. After briefly tracing the origins of this sub-discipline of economics, alternate models of introducing competition in the transport sector are analysed in depth. There are two major forms of competition in transport markets: competition in the market and competition for the market. The first one relates to a situation where markets exist with open entry and exit facility and economic considerations alone being the deciding factor for the scale of operation of a firm. Such a competition in the market scenario could potentially accommodate alternate market structures (monopolistic competition, oligopoly or perfect competition). Competition in a market free from barriers to entry is seen in the provision of many kinds of transport services. For example, goods carriage vehicles and passenger carriage segment while in luxury segment, that is the tourist vehicles, as the product is differentiated with the variation in service quality attributes, monopolistic or oligopolistic markets exist. Where the size of the market is large in comparison to the minimum efficient scale of operation of a mode of transport, several suppliers can operate concurrently at an efficient scale (for example, in trucking and rural bus operations). Where the optimal scale is larger, competition "in the market" can still be effective if there are good modal substitutes (often the case for railways). In such cases, the withdrawal of protective practices, such as route reservation for national carriers or administrative market sharing, while painful in the short run, is often the best basis on which the advantages of competition can be obtained.

Another option is when a regulator wants to introduce competition in the market that is otherwise dominated by the monopoly public sector supplier. Such markets are more common in the developing countries and this competition in the market formulation is the most often resorted to. Competition is introduced in various forms by offering certain routes for the private sector operation, promoting competition among groups and competition between various modes of transport. In such situations, making markets "contestable", through competition for the right to provide subsidized services at least cost, will still allow un remunerative services to be provided at the least real cost. All of these potential hazards of the market process may require qualitative controls (for example, standards for safe operation). Among the ways of introducing competition into the transport markets are route franchising, competition between groups and competition between modes. *Route franchising* is a means of maintaining some public control over the level of services and prices in the public passenger transport market, while using competitive forces to secure supply at the lowest cost. This could be resorted to on un-remunerative bus services as well as for all services with the supplier either carrying only the cost risk or carrying both the cost and revenue risk. *Competition between groups* within a licensed franchise system can be promoted by ensuring that routes for which monopoly franchises are granted overlap sufficiently to encourage competition. This form of competition makes it possible to some degree to organize supply, and limits anti-competitive or chaotic operating practices, so long as there is a strong check against emergence of a single strong cartel. *Competition between modes* can be effective where demand is dense and varied. Some flexibility towards the introduction of new categories of services at higher prices may be a means of reconciling the maintenance of a basic low fare with the provision of varied range of price and quality combinations to meet demand.

Alternate market structures namely perfect competition, monopoly, monopolistic competition and oligopoly are discussed and their relevance in the transport sector are examined. One of the most important tools frequently used in the context of transportation demand estimation is the elasticity of demand. Different concepts of elasticity like price elasticity and cross elasticity are discussed and their application in the transport context explored. It is concluded that being a measure of demand effects of changes in fares or service levels, elasticity of demand provides planners with an efficient tool for assessment of effects of policy measures.

Chapter 3 focuses on the externalities caused by the transport operations. It examines the public good character of the transport infrastructure provision. Discussions in the chapter highlight as to how public good character of the transportational infrastructure often results in market failure in the transport services. The externalities caused due to the transport operation are also examined in the chapter. It is seen that the transport operation causes three major external effects: congestion, accidents, and pollution. These three external effects in turn lead to macro and micro effects in the economy. Congestion defined as the impedance that the vehicles impose on each other in conditions where the transport system approaches its capacity. Indicators used to quantify the level of congestion are discussed and methodology of measuring congestion is reviewed. It is seen that how beginning with Glanville and Smeed (1958), the methodology has improved. While Glanville and Smeed considered only the working time as cost of congestion, Dodgson and Lane (1997) considered working and non working time and DETR (2000) suggested the concept of congestion index and the cost being calculated in terms of changes in the index.

Examining the accidental externalities fundamentals of economics of road safety are discussed. It is often considered to be four dimensional : the cost of accident to the society; willingness of the people to pay to avoid accidents; the macro economic consequences of accidents; and the sharing of liability of an accident. Methodology used in evaluating the ex ante cost of accidents is discussed and its implications in terms of DALY tables is highlighted.

Finally is the issue of environmental externalities caused due to the transport operations. Main pollutants emitted by the motor vehicles are enumerated and their health effects are examined. Mobile sources, particularly motor vehicles, are a major cause of air pollution. Motor vehicles emit CO, HCs, NOx, SO_2, and other toxic substances such as TSP and Pb. Emission rates of CO and HCs from diesel vehicles are lower than that of gasoline vehicles because of better combustion efficiencies. While the emission rate of NOx is higher in diesel vehicles because of lower combustion temperatures. Diesel vehicles emit TSP and higher levels of SO_2 but not Pb. The growing vehicle population is a major contributor to air pollution problems. Initially, these problems were most apparent in city centres but over the last two decades lakes and streams and even remote forests have experienced significant degradation. As evidence of anthropogenic impacts on the upper atmosphere accumulates, there is increasing concern about the part played by motor vehicles in global warming.

With transport externalities being a cause of concern, the policy instruments used worldwide to tackle this problem are discussed in Chapter 4. These are divided under four major classifications: using markets, creating markets, using legislative powers and involving the public. In the first category are the economic instruments of taxes, parking/emission charges, and subsidies. Markets are sought to be created by way of allocation of property rights, privatization and introducing emission trading. The legislative instruments basically rely on the police powers of the state. Often known as command and control instruments, these mainly comprise of prescribing abatement technologies and emission standards. Finally, public involvement in the form of information disclosures and suasive measures has recently become very effective with increased public awareness and spread of information technology.

Adding a totally new dimension to the discussions, Chapter 5 highlights as to how the positive externalities caused due to transport operation in the form of infrastructure facilities, connectivity and increased economic activity could be harnessed for resource mobilization for infrastructural development. The key concerns in road policy namely road construction and maintenance, traffic management, demand management and infrastructure expansion planning and appraisal are examined. Towards the end, theory of road pricing is discussed and the alternate methods used are examined.

One of the often recommended solutions to the transport problems is development of public transport. Owing to its potential of providing a mass rapid transit system at low cost, it is generally recommended as a panacea for most of the transport problems. Chapter 6 is devoted to this important aspect of transport economics. Alternate models of public transport service operation are discussed (public sector operation versus private sector operation) and their pros cons are examined. It is suggested that private sector involvement is essential for provision of efficient services at competitive fares. However, governments need to prepare platform for the private firms to come in. It requires policy formulation in three major areas: price regulations, quality standards and access regulations. Towards the end, the mass rapid transport systems are discussed.

By now the basic framework of important issues is laid down. We are now in a position to talk about formulating a transport policy which keeps the important aspects of transport operation: transport demand management, elasticity of demand, external effects of transport, the various instruments used to mitigate the negative effects of transport, ways to generate resources through transport infrastructure use and promoting public transport. The motto is to promote sustainable transport. Chapter 7 handles this important issue of examining the issues involved in transport policy formulation and sustainable transport provision. The key concerns in transport policy formulation are examined while discussing the guiding principles of Sustainable Transport Policy.

Having discussed and evaluated the key theoretical concepts in transport economics, now is the turn to practically use them in evaluation and formulation of a policy. Under the scanner is the transport policy of Himachal Pradesh – one of the states in the Indian Union. Chapter 8 highlights discussions in this important aspect. Starting with road infrastructure creation in the state, discussions focus on the current policy regime and the key areas of concern in the transport sector. From the key areas, agenda for a new policy is drawn keeping the sustainability aspect in focus.

Chapter 9 is the case study on Himachal Pradesh Transport Department effort to computerize the working of the department and using it as a tool for change management. E-governance maturity model by Backus is used to evaluate the achievements. The pre-project scenario is presented to see how an e-governance project sanctioned by the Department of Information Technology Government of India is used to transform the working in the sector.

Chapter 10 gives conclusions of the study.

2

MICRO-FOUNDATIONS OF TRANSPORT ECONOMICS

2.1 Introduction

Transport refers to the movement of people and goods between destinations and the discipline of *Transport economics* studies the *allocation of resources* used to move passengers and freight from place to place. Transport systems help overcome the effects of distance. They also have the effect of increasing the size of the market by enabling domestic goods to be sold globally, enhance opportunities for international trade and the benefits or economic integration, enabling of Just in Time production techniques (Components are delivered when needed reducing a firm's stock levels hence unit costs), improving mobility of labour (workers can live many miles from work and commute) and improved competitiveness: efficient transport systems minimize travel times and so lower domestic unit costs. Transport operations refer to decisions about what type of transport mode to use or provide. These decisions fall into two main categories- "demand side" and "supply side": *Demand side decisions* are about what journey to make, by what mode, and at what time are taken by consumers and firms, while the *Supply side decisions* concern what transport mode to provide.

The need for mobility is one that dominates the developed and developing countries alike as it helps in improving social welfare. Inadequacy of infrastructure for transportation of goods and passengers is often attributed as one of the key reasons for lower growth rates in the developing countries. As all sectors of the economy require the input of transportation, the transport demand is a derived demand as the determining factor of mobility and modal split are as a result of decision making process elsewhere in the economy. Examples of such factors include production and trade structures, production sites, consumer and dwelling locations, and sites of offices and factories. An interesting fact about transport is that the transport flows occur in the whole chain from the origin of raw materials through the production and distribution process towards the final consumption. It is in the course of these decision making processes that the technical and economic demands made of the transport processes are defined. It results in a two way relationship: service features offered by the different modes also affect the agents demanding transport services (this is particularly relevant in the matter of logistics, outsourcing and market-sizing), and the demand patterns of the production units defines the nature of transport services.

There can be many reasons for inclusion of transport within the chain from production to consumption for instance location of origins of raw materials (where oil is drilled or found) and the climate (where oranges grow). The location of production units may also be affected by the price of production factors. For example, the shift to production to the regions with lower labour costs; technical skills in some cases can restrict production to certain areas and lead to specialization. Economies of scale influence production locations supported by logistical concepts for distribution. Hence all this generates transport flows as a part of the production as well as consumption process.

Being an input in other economic activities, transport raises cost of production and distribution thus requiring transport flows to be optimized (this is where transport economics comes into being). This optimization has to take into account the direct transport costs and other cost factors such as capital costs of the transported goods (time related cost of transporting precious goods). Transport costs including these additional elements are called "generalized transport costs" (Mayeres 2003). Optimization of prices with reference to transport has twin implications. First, it requires both production and delivery processes to be efficient, and cost effective. From the standpoint of a transport service provider, it requires that the selection of mode of service (the vehicle used) is optimal and the delivery of service (the management part) is cost effective. Second, the optimization requirement is little more rigorous. The prices should take into consideration the external effects also.

It is often argued (Mayeres 2003) that pricing in transport is not optimal as these do not often take external effects (like the environmental effects) into account. A change in the price level of transport would have an impact on the process of optimizing production and distribution. Pricing is also an instrument in the policy towards mode choice. Changes in the price levels between modes, on top of changes in the use of modes, will lead to changes in the production and distribution patterns and thereby have an influence on the volumes of transport and transport distances. There is also a correlation between transport and the economy in the opposite direction. Transport facilities are a condition for the functioning of the economic system and can be an incentive to develop further activities in a region. Without transport, no materials from different origins could be assembled and no specialization could take place. The influence of transport facilities (e.g. infrastructure) on the economy is called an indirect effect.

Variation in prices affects demand for transport services. The effect is on demand in short run as well as in the long run. Long run effects occur due to time lag and are often not taken into account properly. With the variation in prices of transport among different modes, analyzing variations in modes becomes a tedious job. Most services being substitutes to each other, variations in prices of one service leads to changes in demand for another service. For example, an increase in prices of passenger fares of bus services results in increase in demand for para transit services. Hence, the concept of cross elasticites of demand assumes significance in transport economics.

Discussions in this chapter revolve around the basic concepts of economics as applied to transport economics. Starting with a brief review on development of transport economics, the forms of competition in the transport markets are examined. It is followed by kinds of markets in transport sector and the concept of elasticity of demand and its relevance in transport economics. It is seen that most markets in the transport context resemble contestable markets, monopolistic competition and oligopolistic structures. Different modes and segments have their own peculiar features giving rise to a particular form of market structure.

2.2 Transport Economics in Historical Perspective

Emphasis in transport economics (both in theory and practice) has shifted from non-market allocation to competition and market oriented provision. The recent shift happened as a move away from neglect of the market in transport since about 1930. The neglect of market forces in transport, for almost fifty years from 1930, is attributed to the following factors:

(a) The Keynesian revolution changed the emphasis to macroeconomic management and away from microeconomic issues. The State came to be seen as the key factor in resource allocation rather than the market;

(b) The belief that market forces were inherently unstable and caused the 1929 crash and the 1930s slump;

(c) The success of incumbent producers in the transport sector in achieving regulatory capture over governments at the expense of consumers and new market entrants. Incumbents thus acquired a property right of exemption from normal market forces; and

(d) The concentration of economic expertise in the public service in departments of finance and a neglect of economics in spending departments such as transport.

Transportation and the emergence of nation state played a strategic role in the nineteenth century and was the principle reason for infrastructure provision under the authority of the State. Granting of privileges for infrastructure provision was typical for the state to incorporate private capital with public necessities. The setting of prices was however supervised and, very often the privileges were only granted on the basis of the obligation to also include or access marginal customers. Public good and essential services were sought to be defined by the nation state as being so important and socially valuable that a public provision seemed necessary.

The return of market forces mainly occurred as the gains from deregulation in terms of lower prices and better services forged a link between the advocates of the market forces and consumer interests. The argument that contestability theory implements the welfare gains of perfect competition gained importance. The world of many buyers and many sellers, each one a price taker (production only in response to consumer preferences and carried on by the most efficient firms) is no longer regarded as irrelevant to the real world. Potential new entrants ensure that price tends to remain around the long-run marginal cost and supernormal profits are not earned. Costs are minimized and that the industry always comprises the optimum number of firms. As the emphasis in economics shifted back to markets, the successes of deregulation in terms of gains to consumers and the economy were the decisive validation of contestability theory and the policy of deregulation.

Typically there are two types of competition most prevalent in the transport sector.

(a) Competition in the Market

It is the most natural form of economic competition that occurs in the market giving consumers the benefit of choice. The suppliers are thus forced to be alert and keep a constant vigil on the moves of the consumers in the form of changes in demand which is the biggest factor in stimulating efficiency, cost effectiveness and technological improvements. Competition in a market free from barriers to entry is seen in the provision of many kinds of transport services. For example, goods carriage vehicles and passenger carriage segment while in luxury segment, that is the tourist vehicles, as the product is differentiated with the variation in service quality attributes, monopolistic or oligopolistic markets exist. Where the size of the market is large in comparison to the minimum efficient scale of operation of a mode of transport, several suppliers can operate concurrently at an efficient scale (for example, in trucking and rural bus operations). Where the optimal scale is larger, competition "in the market" can still be effective if there are good modal substitutes (often the case for railways). In such cases, the withdrawal of protective practices, such as route reservation for national carriers or administrative market sharing, while painful in the short run, is often the best basis on which the advantages of competition can be obtained. More generally, free entry may be preferable to the alternative of ineffective or corrupt regulation if indigenous administrative skills are scarce.

However, there are some limitations to it also. It is often argued (World Bank 1996) that the intensity of competition could lead to instability or even rupture of supply. It is particularly seen with reference to the transport services in the urban areas and less often in case of charted services also. The main risks of over competition could be:

- Instability in the market as operators have to constantly change their strategies;
- Duplication of services often results in wastage of resources;
- Over capacity as a result of optimistic vision by too many leading to parallel investments, often underutilized;
- Cherry picking of services with the highest density of demand with better load factor and easy returns. It could leave the other areas un-served.
- There are problems arising out of operational complexities in terms of competition led violation of technical regulations. Instances

of overloading, over speeding, excessive working hours and chasing are commonly seen.

Such situations are rather very common in the developing world which leaves the government to define the market. There are thus cases of allocation of business by the government and restriction imposed on the nature and quantum of services in a particular area. Experience over the years has shown that it is possible to achieve stability in the market through product differentiation or through oligopoly.

(b) Competition for the Market

In case of competition for the market, the public authorities define the kind of transport infrastructure needed by them and the firms compete to maker the supply available. Given the high initial costs and their irreversibility, this is the most common form of introducing competition when infrastructure is to be built, operated and maintained. Owing to its advantages in the form of lower risk of instability and rupture of services, it is the most preferred form in case of competition in the market. There are three distinct reasons why it can be desirable to retain some public regulation of the right to supply transport. First, where *duplication of supply would be either wasteful or impractical*, as with indivisible infrastructures (major highways and bridges), the need to regulate stems from the danger of monopoly exploitation. Second, regulation may be desirable in some cases where an unregulated *market process* may result in: (i) matching of schedules (in local bus markets); (ii) increased pressure to engage in dangerous practices, such as overloading of freight vehicles or racing of buses; and (iii) perceived losses in the stability and reliability of service, with consequential losses in patronage and reductions in vehicle occupancy. Third, while cost reductions resulting from unfettered competition may allow services to continue that were previously unprofitable, and may even lead to more frequent services being provided on previously un remunerative routes by using smaller vehicles more suited to low demand, *social objectives* may require direct financing of some services that might otherwise be lost through competition in the market (for example, connecting the remote areas having limited potential, providing concessional travel to the weaker sections or priority services like services connecting educational institutions or health centres). In such situations, making markets "contestable", through competition for the right to provide subsidized services at least cost, will still allow un remunerative services to be provided at the least real cost. All of these potential hazards of the market process may require qualitative controls (for example, standards for safe operation). However, as is often suggested, it should not be used to promote monopoly franchises or direct state provision of services.

Among the ways of introducing competition into the Transport Market are:

- *Route franchising* is a means of maintaining some public control over the level of services and prices in the public passenger transport market, while using competitive forces to secure supply at the lowest cost. This could be resorted to on un remunerative bus services as well as for all services with the supplier either carrying only the cost risk or carrying both the cost and revenue risk. Where fragmented competition is not possible because of the indivisible scale of operation, market disciplines can still be employed by *concessioning* facilities or systems.

- *Competition between groups* within a licensed franchise system can be promoted by ensuring that routes for which monopoly franchises are granted overlap sufficiently to encourage competition. This form of competition makes it possible to some degree to organize supply, and limits anti-competitive or chaotic operating practices, so long as there is a strong check against emergence of a single strong cartel.
- *Competition between modes* can be effective where demand is dense and varied. Some flexibility towards the introduction of new categories of services at higher prices may be a means of reconciling the maintenance of a basic low fare with the provision of varied range of price and quality combinations to meet demand.

World Bank (2002) highlights how all service operation can be undertaken by the private sector in some form (Table 2.1).

Table 2.1 : Expanding the Scope for Private Sector in Transport

	Infrastructure	*Services*
Urban road	Though usually free, access expressways and bridges can be tolled;	All should be private sector, with free entry competitive franchising in the bus market, according to local circumstance. Barriers to entry of the informal sector could be reduce.
Inter-urban road	Usually public owned but construction and maintenance should normally be contracted out to private sector. Concession development of high traffic volume toll roads and commercialization of public road agencies possible for major roads.	Trucking and inter-city buses could be entirely private with free competition in the market.
Rural road	Scope for commercialization limited by low traffic volumes, transaction costs and social objectives. Construction and maintenance could	Buses, non-motorized transport (NMT) and trucking could all be exclusively private with free entry to the market.

Technological innovations are lowering the barriers to entry by reducing the sunk costs even though the incumbents are developing their ways to block competition by resorting to predatory prices and cartelization.

2.3 Market Structures in Transport Supply

(a) Perfect Competition

The models of perfect competition provide a benchmark illustrating the limiting case of a market involving a very high level of competition. It is assumed that there is a large number of firms and consumers so that neither producers nor consumers can affect the price of the posited undifferentiated product. It is also assumed that there is free entry into and exit from the market, implying no entry or exit barriers. The cost and revenue conditions for an individual supplier (firm) in a perfectly competitive market in the long run are illustrated in Table 2.1. As much as the seller wishes can be sold at the price P. Each additional unit of output is sold for the same price. Therefore the extra revenue which the producer obtains from selling every additional unit of output, the marginal revenue, is equal to the price and is also equal to the average revenue from selling each unit of output. A cost structure is assumed where both the marginal cost of producing each additional unit and average cost per unit first decrease as output rises and then increase owing, initially, to increasing returns to scale and subsequently to decreasing returns. Producers are unwilling to produce for a price less than the prevailing market price, P as they would make a loss. Hence, the section o the marginal cost curve to the right of Q is the producer's supply curve, since it shows the quantity of output which the producer would like to supply at each price in the short run. Effectively, this means that the quantity supplied will be increased only if prices rise.

The optimal point of production from the supplier's viewpoint occurs where the marginal cost is equal to the marginal revenue,

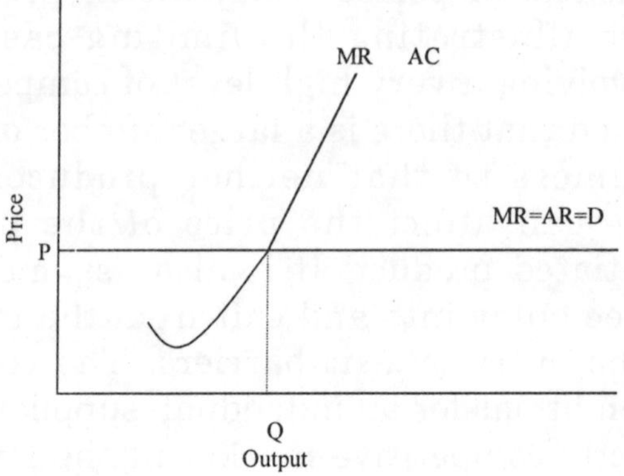

Figure: 2: Production by a firm in a perfectly competitive market

P=Price, Q= quantity of output, MC- marginal cost, AC= average cost, MR=marginal revenue, AR= average revenue, D=demand

corresponding to an output, Q, in Figure 2. This is the point at which profits are maximized, as can easily be demonstrated numerically. Output below Q is associated with marginal revenue in excess of marginal cost, so that producers wish to increase production because they can increase profits. Conversely, at levels of output above Q, marginal revenue is less than marginal cost so that producers experience reduced profit and would seek to decrease production to the profit maximizing level of output. Hence, the supply curve for the industry is horizontal at the price, P over the long run. If costs were to increase, for example, fuel became more expensive, producers with higher average costs would go out of business if they are just breaking even at output Q, that is, earning only normal profits. An overall decrease in costs would result in a short run outcome of supernormal profits which would attract more producers into the industry until profits returned to their normal level. Thus, within a perfectly competitive market, the prevailing price may result in supernormal profits or losses in the short run. However, there is tendency towards a break-even price, equal to marginal cost where average cost is at a minimum, and consumers appear to benefit. This raises the issue of whether the permit regime in various segments should be liberalized to increase competition whereby supernormal profits are earned should be rendered more competitive and whether this would increase consumers' welfare. There is no unequivocal answer because, in the context of economies of scale where an increase in the firm's output is accompanied by a fall in the average cost of each unit of production, it is possible for imperfectly competitive markets to be more efficient than those under perfect competition.

(b) Contestable Markets

It has been argued that although most real world markets are not perfectly competitive, a significant number give rise to similar economic outcomes. Baumol (1982) introduced the concept of contestability to take account of this outcome. A contestable market is characterized by insignificant entry and exit costs, so that there are negligible entry and exit barriers. Sunk cost, which a firm incurs in order to produce and which would not be recoverable it the firm left the industry, are not significant. Because of reasonably efficient information flows, the same supply conditions and technology are available to all producers. It is assured that producers are unable to change prices instantaneously but consumers react to them immediately. The key insight of contestability is that new and existing firms find it possible to challenge the position of rivals through pricing strategies. Thus, firms in contestable markets operate similarly to those perfectly competitive markets in that they charge approximately the same price for a given product. Although economies of scale and scope may arise, incumbent firms are unable to charge a price exceeding average cost because this would attract competitors into the market. Rivals would not be averse to entry because of the low sunk costs and low entry/exist barriers. Hence, contestable markets may be beneficial to consumers. Markets in Goods Carriage segment and Stage Carriage vehicles segment fall in this category.

(c) Monopoly

Monopoly represents the opposite extreme of perfect competition. Unlike producers in a perfectly competitive market, the monopolist has considerable control over the product price and level of output. Given normal demand conditions, in order to sell additional output, the product price must be lowered so that average revenue falls and consequently the marginal revenue per additional unit of output sold decreases as the amount sold rises. The relationship between the two forms of revenue is such that marginal revenue decreases by twice as much as the average revenue and hence the marginal revenue curve lies below the average revenue curve, as illustrated in Figure-3. Following economic suppositions regarding cost structures, returns increase and then decrease; therefore the marginal and average cost curves initially decline and subsequently rise.

Profits are maximized at a level of output where the marginal cost of production equals the marginal revenue and marginal cost is

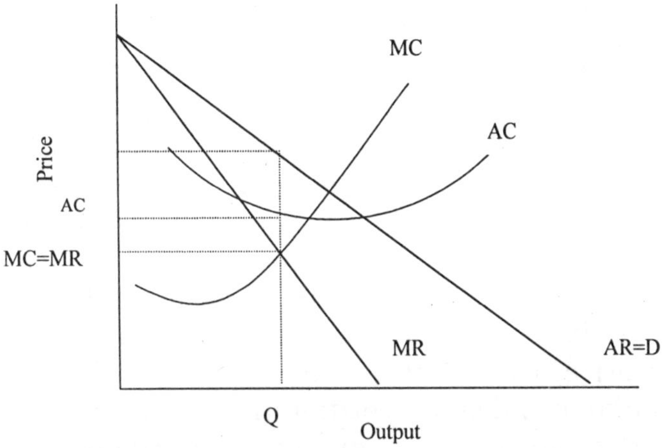

Figure: 3: Production by a monopoly

P=Price, Q= quantity of output, MC- marginal cost, AC= average cost, MR=marginal revenue, AR= average revenue, D=demand

rising (or in cases where increasing returns prevail, marginal cost is falling less rapidly than marginal revenue). As is shown in figure-3, the average cost of production is lower than the price charged giving rise to supernormal profits, above the minimum required to keep the firm in the industry. Thus, consumers are paying a price in excess of that which might emerge in a more competitive market. This raises the issue of whether the monopoly should be allowed to trade unhindered or be regulated or reorganized as competitive industry (it is being resorted to in case of public sector monopolies in stage carriage segment), models of competition for the market are being introduced in various parts of the country.

However, two interesting outcomes may occur under monopoly as opposed to competition, which illustrate the debate concerning the relative advantages and disadvantages of each type of market structure. The first case involves a comparison of the equilibrium price and output combinations under competition and monopoly respectively, in which it is assumed that a competitive industry is monopolized without any change in production conditions. The outcome is illustrated in Figure-4, which assumes that each competitive firm can be excluded. It is clear that the price, P1, is lower and the quantity produced, Q, higher under competition than under monopoly. If the industry were monopolized, profit maximization would occur where the short-run marginal cost, SMC, is equal to the marginal revenue, MR, resulting in a higher price, P_2 and lower output, Q_2. In the long run, the monopolist could close some production units, decreasing output to Q_3 and increasing the price to P_3. Thus, consumers would be worse off under monopoly than under competitive conditions. Industry where small independent, bus, coach or ferry operators are amalgamated as, to an extent, has occurred with deregulation; after an initial influx of new entrants, larger enterprises have taken over many of the smaller firms and exercised monopoly powers.

In the second case, production conditions differ according to whether the industry is operated as a monopoly or under competition as large economies of scale can apply when production is undertaken by a singe firm. This applies in the case of a so-called natural monopoly in which both the marginal and average costs are lower over the range of output which could be purchased in comparison with competition. In these circumstances, consumers benefit in terms of a lower price and higher quantity of production even if the monopolist made supernormal profits. However, a government would need to subsidize production since the price would be lower than the average cost of production, so that supplier makes a loss. For example, most rail systems operate at a loss in terms of not covering average total costs because they are viewed as providing to charge prices at which they endeavour to cover operating (marginal) costs and contribute to meeting fixed costs. Even if the monopoly were not regulated consumers might benefit, in the long run, from product and process innovations resulting from the reinvestment of some of the profits gained by the monopolist, including the necessary research and development. Under competitive conditions, the availability of funding for research and development is sometimes problematic.

The difficulty of predicting determined outcome can be aptly illustrated by the examples of state-sanctioned monopoly rail and airline markets. Many governments partially or totally privatized a number of services, which were hitherto perceived as natural monopolies. The rationale has often been that, notwithstanding economic scale, they could be operated more efficiently as private sector industries. Privatization has often been accompanied by deregulation to encourage new entrants and increase competition. However, paradoxically, the eventual effect has often been to bring about greater concentration. One important reason is that smaller new entrants are unable fully to exploit economies of scale and therefore fail. It is still too early to establish empirically what the structure of the airline, bus, ferry or rail sector will be. Effective regulation may be needed to prevent abuses of monopoly power in the form of high prices and the extraction of usually define monopoly as occurring when a single producer accounts for a specific, relatively high percentage of production of a particular product and monitor the operations of the firm in question in an attempt to ensure that consumers are not disadvantaged.

(d) Monopolistic Competition

Monopolistic competition is a type of market structure, often associated with retailing, is intermediate between perfect competition and monopoly. It is similar to that of perfect competition and contestable markets in that there is ease of entry and exist in the long run. However, it differs in that suppliers have some control over the price which they sell their product and, thus, also over their price/output combination and associated market share. However, the pricing and output decisions of an individual supplier do not have a significant impact on those of another because it is normally assumed that there are many suppliers who provide products which are close but not exact substitutes, so that there is some degree of product differentiation reinforced, as in retailing, by the spatial separation and location of businesses.

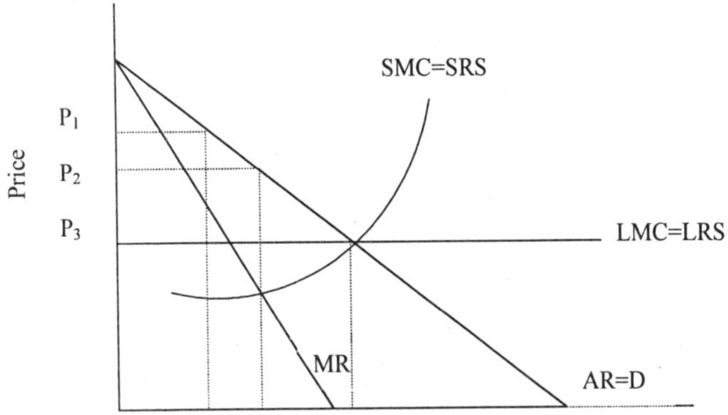

Figure: 4: Short-run and long-run production by a perfectly competitive industry and a monopoly

Note: P=price, Q=quantity of output, SMC=short-run marginal cost, LMC= long-run marginal cost, SRS= short-run supply, LRS= long-run supply, MR= marginal revenue, AR= average revenue, D=demand

In the short run, suppliers within a monopolistically competitive market can charge a price which provides them with supernormal profit. Firms produce where their short-run marginal revenue, SMR, is equal to their marginal cost and charge a price which exceeds their average cost, as illustrated by the price and output combination, P_1 and Q_1 in Figure- 4. However, in the long run, supernormal profits, combines with the virtual absence of entry and exit barriers for the industry, attract new competitors so that existing firms experience a decline in the demand for their products. This is illustrated by shift to the left of the average revenue (demand) curve, SAR, and the short run marginal revenue curve, SMR, until they attain their long run positions, given by LAR and LMR with an equilibrium price P_2 and output Q_2.

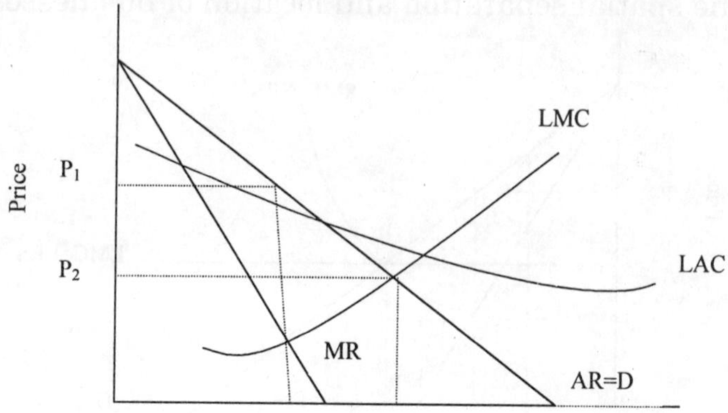

Figure: 5: Long-run production by an unregulated and regulated natural monopoly

Note: P=price, Q=quantity of output, LMC=long-run marginal cost, LAC=long-run average cost, MR=marginal revenue, AR=average revenue, D=demand

Over the long run, demand decreases until the break-even point where average revenue, shown as the price P_2 is equal to the average cost of production so that there is no further entry into (or exit from) the industry. Although output has contracted and supernormal profits have disappeared, the price charged is still greater than the marginal cost of production. Hence this form of competition appears less efficient that perfect competition although the wide variety of products provides consumers with greater variety of choice. There are a number of examples of transport business in this position such as the smaller firms in the contestable segments of the tourist transport operators, where the extent of their market limits the possibilities of operating at a level which reduces their costs. This might explain why smaller airlines, bus and ferry operators eventually get taken over as they cannot compete at prevailing prices, especially during a price war.

(e) Oligopoly

An oligopolistic market structure occurs when a small number of firms dominate the industry. The international airline industry being a case in point. Each firm has some control over its price and output decisions and there are some barriers to entry and exit. The key characteristic of oligopoly is the interdependence between producers so that each firm's price and output decisions depend, in part, on those of its competitors. One well-known example of such interdependence, which has become a standard case in economic, is that of the oligopolist's perceived kinked demand curve, which shows the likely outcome for a firm, should it contemplate a change in its price in the absence of changes in cost or demand conditions which affect the whole of the industry. It knows that if it decreases its price its competitors will follow suit, demand for its own prices so its demand is more elastic and it will close market share. Thus, the prevailing market price is the profit-maximizing price for the firm.

Ideally, individual oligopolists prefer prices to be set at a level which maximizes the joint profits of all producers in the industry. In effect, if all the firms in the industry could act together, the result would be similar to a monopolist, leading to an increase in price and a decrease in the quantity sold, in contrast to the outcome that would occur under competitive conditions, as previously demonstrated in Figure 5. The possibility of obtaining supernormal profits by this means provides a rationale for inter-firm collusion. For example, inter airline pricing and route sharing agreements have been one example of a strategy which has been used to increase joint profits. On the other hand, there is an incentive for an individual firm to cheat as, if it could do so successfully, it would increase its profits and market share relative to those of its competitors. The stability of a number of pricing and output sharing arrangements may be accounted for by the fact that should all firms cheat, all would be likely to be worse off.

2.4 Elasticity of Demand in Transport

(a) Price Elasticity of Demand

The term elasticity is used extensively in economics and transport economics. The concept is simple and straightforward. Elasticity of demand is defined as the percentage change in quantity consumed that is caused by a percentage change in a determinant of demand. Price elasticity of demand for example, is a convenient way of comparing how price changes affect the quantity consumed. It is the ratio of two percentages – the change in quantity consumed that results from a change in price. When the percentage change in price results in a larger percentage change in quantity demanded, the demand is said to be elastic. By elastic we mean that the quantity demanded is quite sensitive or very responsive to price changes. Conversely, when the percentage change in price results in a smaller percentage in quantity demanded it is said to be inelastic (the quantity is not very sensitive to changes in the price).

When elasticity is multiplied by an expected percentage change in a variable, it is given an estimate of the expected percentage change in demand. Thus, it is clear that estimates of elasticities of demand can play an important role in understanding the consequences of socioeconomic trends and management alternatives. Applied in case of transport it implies for instance an increase in fares by 5 percent with a fare elasticity of -0.4 brings a passenger loss of 1.9 percent. There are different concepts of elasticity applied in economics. If the case under consideration is the change in demand for a good from changes in the price of the same good, it is called as own price elasticity. However, if the effect of change in price of one good is considered on the demand of another good, it is called as cross elasticity. For example change in demand for public transport when the prices of car or fuel rise.

Price elasticity of demand is a measure of the responsiveness of quantity demanded to changes in the direct cost or price of trips to a recreation site, holding constant the values of all other variables. The general formula for the price elasticity follows from its definition:

$$\text{Price} = \frac{\text{Percent change in quantity}}{\text{Percent change in price}}$$

$$= \frac{\text{Change in quantity} - \text{Original quantity}}{\text{Change in price} - \text{Originalprice}}$$

The price elasticity of demand will always be negative, since price and quantity change in opposite directions. Thus, an elasticity of -1.0 is greater than an elasticity of -0.5, and an elasticity of -2.0 is greater than an elasticity of -1.0.

There are many equivalent formulas for calculating the elasticity of demand and the choice among them will depend on the information available to you. First, if we have access to a linear demand function, by algebraically rearranging the above equation to estimate the price elasticity of demand for any point on the demand curve using the following formula:

$$\text{Price elasticity} = \frac{\Delta Q}{\Delta P} \times \frac{P_o}{Q_o}$$

The first expression in this formula, change in quantity demanded divided by change in price, is equivalent to the regression coefficient for price. Thus, the formula can be rewritten as:

$$\text{Price elasticity} = \text{Regression coefficient for price} \times \frac{P_o}{Q_o}$$

The regression coefficient for direct cost or price per trip is shown in above equation as -0.1. The average direct cost or price is shown as Rs. 20 per trip; at this price, the representative individual user takes five trips per year. If we insert these values in the forumula:

Price elasticity = $-0.1 \times \text{Rs.}\frac{20}{5} = -0.4$

Thus, dividing the original price (Rs.20) by the original quantity demanded (5 trips) equals 4, and multiplying this by the regression coefficient (-0.1) equals price elasticity of demand. This means that a 1 percent increase in price from the original level results in a 0.4 percent decrease in quantity demanded, or conversely for a price decrease. Now you are familiar with the preferred procedure when statistical demand functions are available; however, this may not always be the case.

Measuring price elasticities in the transport sector is a complex problem and has therefore been the focus of much research. The results are wide-ranging as elasticity is highly contingent on individual cases. As transport is an intermediate good (people do not travel and goods are not shipped for the sake of mobility but for a specific purpose or end product), the overall elasticity of transport depends on the usefulness of the end product. The price elasticities of each mode of transport depend on the availability of competing modes, as well as on service quality (journey time, comfort, safety) in the relevant mode — and all of these factors vary from one practical situation to another. It is important to look at the insight to be gained from the leading studies on elasticities, and the many reviews of that literature. The best known reviews were conducted some years ago by Oum *et al.*(1992) and Goodwin (1992). These broad studies were later supplemented by other works with a more specific focus, in particular statistical meta-analyses, designed to reveal the basic parameters governing elasticities.

(b) Cross Elasticity of Demand

Besides the direct cost or price of a trip and the level of consumer income, the demand for transport for a particular mode also depends on the price of other related mode. Cross elasticity of demand is used to measure the sensitivity of the former's demand to changes in the latter's price. Cross elasticity is defined as the percent change in the quantity demanded of one good or service resulting from a one percent change in the price of another good or service. A distinction needs to be made between own price elasticities, that is the impact that a change in the price of a mode – or sub-mode – has on traffic in that mode; cross-price elasticities, that is the impact that a change in the price of a mode – or sub-mode – has on traffic in a competing mode; and elasticities with respect to the other parameters governing traffic (journey time, service quality, level of economic activity).

Pairs of goods and services are classified as substitutes or complements depending on whether the cross elasticity of demand is positive or negative. If the cross elasticity of demand is positive, two goods or services are substitutes because a decrease in the price of one, for example, will result in a decrease in the demand for another. On the other hand, if the cross elasticity of demand is negative, two goods or services are complements. For example, petrol and cars may be complements since an increase in the price of petrol will decrease the demand for cars. When cross elasticity of demand is zero, or nearly zero, we can conclude that the goods or services are unrelated and in separate and distinct markets. Variations in the price of one good or service would have no effect on demand for the second.

With reference to cross price elasticity of inter-modal services, cross-elasticities are rather difficult to interpret, as they reflect not only inter-modal substitution but also the market share weighting of individual modes. Any conclusions necessarily reflect that weighting, and in fact reveal very little modal transfer. Taking the own-price elasticity of -0.7, a 10 per cent increase in road transport prices would result in 7 per cent fall in road traffic and of that 7 percent, 1.5 percent would shift to rail while 5.5 percent would disappear.

In the context of transport economics, the elasticity effects are studied in terms of their short run and long run effects due to a price change. There is an increasing evidence that short run effects are just a small fraction of long run effects. In the short run most passengers have few alternatives to the services they are dependent on. However, in the long run, it is possible to respond fully to the changes by making fundamental changes in the demand and modal split. For example, changes in fares may force the households to shift dwelling accommodations near the work places, change their car ownership status or even change the job itself. Several studies indicate that long run effects are in the region of 1.5 to 3 times the short run effects. Very often due to the non-availability of data, the transport planners are only able to take into consideration the short run effects.

2.5 Conclusion

Transport systems exist not only in themselves but as a critical supplier of services to the people and the economic agents thus making their predictability, stability and efficiency important for the economy as a whole. Cheaper technologies and communication are moving towards more efficient allocation of capacity, pricing systems and demand responsive mechanisms. It has substantially improved the flexibility and integration of services in the market. However, it is a dynamic game with the private parties always trying to penetrate in the market and improve their share in the market. The technological improvements also make the dynamics more interesting. The authorities are therefore required to be more pragmatic and flexible in keeping the market requirements. It raises the need for redesigning policies and their instruments including making it necessary for the authorities to become learning institutions.

Demand elasticities are of vital importance for anyone engaged in transport planning and management. Being a measure of demand effects of changes in for example fares or service levels, elasticities provide planners with an efficient tool for assessment of many policy measures. Overall, economic activity elasticities are around +1 for passenger transport and +1.5 for freight. There are fewer studies on service quality, probably because it is not easy to gauge and because reliable statistics on the subject are harder to find.

3
EXTERNAL EFFECTS OF TRANSPORT

3.1 Introduction

Public good and externalities are the two important features that make public provision of transport infrastructure necessary. *A public good is generally considered as a good that, once provided for one consumer, can be generally made available to other consumers and firms at no extra cost* (Karpagam 1991). Thus by definition these goods are characterized by non-excludability and non-rival consumption. For reasons of physical impossibility and financial prudence, it is not possible to exclude anybody from enjoying the benefits of it. However, non-excludability is not the only feature, which makes a public good; non-rival consumption is another reason for it. Non-rival consumption implies that its provision to any one individual entails its provision to another individual who can consume the same unit at the same time. The best example of the public good is the defence of the country. It involves maximum externality of consumption as its benefits accrue automatically and simultaneously to the entire population of the country. The free access to the public goods often results in their overuse. Owing to these features of non-excludability and non-rival consumption, the markets do not function as it is very difficult to charge appropriate price for these resources.

External effects have been studied by the economists ever since the days of Marshall and Pigou. Along with the development of the field of environmental economics, the theory of externalities has remained of great and growing importance in economic science. Verhoef (1999) believes that it is fair to say that starting from the traditional neoclassical economic framework, the most logical way to look at environmental problems is from the point of view of external cost (Baumol and Oates 1988; Pearce and Turner 1990; Cropper and Oates 1992; Tietenberg 1995). In an economic context, externality is caused by activities that not only affect the buyer and the seller, but also yield incidental benefits or cause incidental injuries to the parties not directly involved in exchange. These unintended side effects are called '*externalities*' (Baumol and Oates, 1988). The discharge of polluted water by an industrial unit into the inland water causes 'externality effect' as the cost of loss of human well-being caused due to this discharge is not borne by the unit. Alternatively, damage inflicted by one agent has inevitable repercussions for various other economic agents as well, and that it is difficult to exclude one from being affected by the damage. Therefore, owing to lack of excludability, the costs cannot be reflected in actual and potential market exchanges.

It is commonly recognized that externalities are an important form of market failure (Verhoef 1999). Their existence leads to a deviation from the first-best neoclassical world, in which the price mechanism takes care of an efficient resource allocation. In the presence of externalities, market prices do not reflect full social costs or benefits, and, for instance, regulatory taxes or subsidies are called for to restore the efficient workings of the market mechanism. It is often argued that the source of externalities is typically to be found in the absence of well defined property rights (Baumol and Oates 1988). Consequently, the theory of externalities is often applied in environmental economics, for instance, environmental quality is a typical good for which property rights are not defined and hence no markets exists. In terms of Verhoef (1999), an external effect exists when an actor's utility (or production) function contains real variable whose actual value depends on the behaviour of another actor, who doesn't take this effect of his behaviour into account in his decision-making process.

Discussions in this chapter focus on analyzing the externalities caused due to transport operation and the policy issues involved in their management.

3.2 The Theoretical Framework

Transportation produces external effects in the form of pollution, congestion and road accidents. These externalities cause market failure in transport. The problem could be depicted graphically. On the horizontal axis in the Figure-7, we measure the number of vehicles at a certain point of time often referred to as mobility. The marginal benefit curve is the demand curve for mobility. Given a certain number of vehicles, it gives the maximum price the marginal road user is willing to pay for driving. The marginal benefit curve is decreasing assuming that different individuals receive different levels of utility by driving. For a very high price of transport, only those individuals with a high marginal benefit will drive, but as the cost of transport decreases, the number of individuals finding it worthwhile to drive will presumably increase. The marginal private cost curve is the equivalent of the supply curve. Using a vehicle to commute at a certain time involves cost like gasoline cost, and maintenance cost. If these were the only cost of mobility, the marginal cost curve would be horizontal as all individuals spend the same amount for mobility. However, it is not so in the real world situation as the road space is a resource common to all drivers and it has capacity constraints, as the number of vehicles on road increases, the congestion cost in the form of time consumed in travel increases making the marginal cost curve rising upwards as the volume of traffic increases.

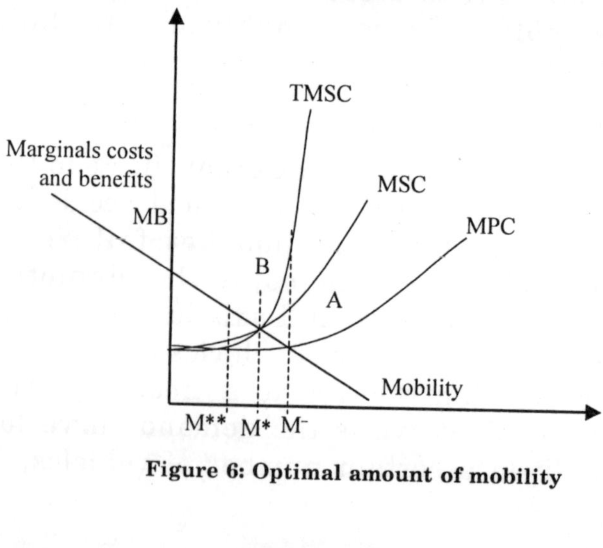

Figure 6: Optimal amount of mobility

With the addition of an additional vehicle on the road, as the congestion increases, it not only increases the travel time of the driver of a particular car but also has external effect of increasing the travel time of the previous car. Thus the marginal social cost comes into being. As the microeconomic analysis suggests, the optimum level of mobility should be determined by the intersection of marginal benefit curve and the marginal social cost curve. In practice the individual driver will disregard the marginal social cost of travel and will keep moving till the marginal private cost is equal to the marginal benefit of travel. A policy that allows reduction of mobility from M' to M* maximizes social welfare. While if the other externalities in the form of pollution and accidents are also taken into account, the Total Marginal Social Cost Curve (TMSC) takes the optimum level of mobility to even lower level at M** .

Owing to the external effects, the transportation system services fail to take into account the social cost of their operation. For example, as a bus emits smoke that increases the level of SPM in the area thus increasing morbidity around this cost of negative externality is not reflected in its cost of operation. It is also possible that the cost of smoke reducing device is far cheaper than the laundry bill, yet since the unit is not made to internalize the cost of pollution it causes, there is no incentive for the bus to install the abatement equipment. Therefore, the passenger fares charged do not reflect the true cost of operation. The operation may appear to be cheaper and the bus will operate more number of trips because of the implicit subsidy that occurs when others pay part of the cost of operation. The bus company thus experiences increasing returns to scale and tends to produce more and pollute more. The production function of the company in this case will be concave instead of the normal convex one. Where such spill over occur, the private enterprise system will respond imperfectly to the desires of the public and the output will also be undesirably large; it will exceed far more than what it would have been if the firm was made to internalize the cost of damage they inflict on the environmental resources or the local population.

Although scientific knowledge about environmental processes has advanced substantially over the past two decades, global environmental problems still remain subject of substantial uncertainty. For instance, scientific controversy over the greenhouse effect is still raging, and even if it is accepted as a matter of scientific fact its economic implications remain highly uncertain (Karshenas 1994). At the local level also, we are not sure about the exact causes and effects of so many environmental problems and the appropriate solutions for them. The abatement technologies are equally complex and too large in number making it further difficult to select the appropriate technology. To state in the words of Baumol and Oates (1988), when the automobile began to replace the horse and rid the streets of odorous dung heaps, it was hailed as a major contributor to public health and sanitation, however, soon came the revelation that the automobiles are responsible for most of the man-made carbon monoxide in the atmosphere, and half of hydrocarbons, half of nitrogen oxide, and in an area where there are no industries that produce or use lead, about 90 percent of air borne lead pollution.

Complexities of scientific processes and technological know how create wide spread information failure in the market. The information asymmetries arise on three fronts. Firstly, the consumer does not know the environmental information of the product. Secondly, the producers are not aware of the environmental costs of their operations, the appropriate technologies and the abatement equipments. Finally, the geographical and inter-temporal implications of both production and consumption are not known.

Information asymmetries cause twin problems: adverse selection and moral hazard. Both adverse selection and moral hazard, at their core, are information problems. Information asymmetry arises when information is available to only one side of a market leading to market failure. Neither would arise if there were a free flow of information. Lack of information often leads to *adverse selection*. Adverse selection in the transport context is a manifestation of a situation where the service provider is aware of the external effects of the operation, but is able to conceal it from the users (for example, plying a vehicle without the same being mechanically fit for roads). With information being seriously deficient, market outcomes may be less satisfactory. Markets are generally more efficient when (a) the better is consumer informed, (b) more cheaply and effectively it can be improved, (c) the easier it is for the consumers to understand available information, (d) the lower are the costs of choosing badly, and (e) the more diverse are the consumer tastes. Commodities that conform well to these criterions are, for instance, food and such consumer durables like personal computers.

Moral hazard raises a different set of efficiency problems. It arises where the damages caused by a vehicle to the society are insured by the insurance company so that the firm has no incentive to mitigate the damage. More complete the cover and the lower the psychic loss from the insured event, the less firms have to bear the consequences of their action and less therefore the incentive to behave as they would if they had to bear the loss themselves. Another form of moral hazard arises when the insured person can influence the expected loss at a cost lower than the expected gain. Despite the insurance cover requiring the firm to invest in preventive activities, thereby reducing the probability of occurrence of the insured event, if the losses are fully insured and the insurance company cannot monitor individual preventive activities, the extra spending by a firm reduces its premium marginally. As a result of this type of externality, firms face private incentive to under invest in preventive activities. When markets are incomplete, risk must be endogenous: the individual might privately influence many of the environmental risks he or she confronts. Examples of endogenous risk in which the individual can choose to alter outcomes abound. People move to reduce physical activities when air pollution becomes intolerable. They buy bottled water if they suspect that the supplies are polluted.

3.3 Externalities from Road Transport

The externalities caused due the transport operation are of two kinds: positive and negative. The positive externalities arise as a result of public good character of the transport infrastructure. For example construction of roads facilitates transportation of goods and services and hence generate external economies to the economic units. The negative externalities occur in the form of congestion, pollution and road accidents.

(a) Congestion

Congestion is defined as the impedance vehicles impose on each other, due to the speed-flow relationship, in conditions where the use of a transport system approaches its capacity. This definition indicates that the underlying *cause* of congestion does not consist of the transient and immediate triggers which drivers notice when they are in a traffic queue, such as road works or taxis or accidents: the cause is because traffic flows are too close to capacity, when any of these transient incidents will have a disproportionate effect. The more traffic using a road, the slower it goes, the effect becoming more and more severe as the traffic flow approaches the maximum capacity of the network until, finally, overload is so extreme that all vehicles are unable to move. For calculation of cost, the idea of travel time is extended to a wider definition of cost, including inconvenience and discomfort. Thus, congestion is a characteristic of all heavily used transport systems. Its general feature is that users impede each other's freedom of movement.

A vehicle's road space requirements increase with speed, because drivers must leave more distance between their vehicle and other objects on or beside the roadway. Traffic flow (the number of vehicles that can travel on a road over a particular time period) tends to be maximized at 30-55 mph on highways with no intersections, and at even lower speeds on arterials with signalized intersections. When a roadway approaches its maximum capacity, even small speed reduction can significantly increase flow rates.

Traffic congestion is a non-linear function, meaning that a small reduction in urban-peak traffic volume can cause a proportionally larger reduction in delay. For example, a 5 percent reduction in traffic volumes on a congested highway (for example, from 2,000 to 1,900 vehicles per hour) may cause a 10-30 percent increase in average vehicle speeds (for example, increasing traffic speeds from 35 to 45 miles per hour). As a result, even relatively small changes in traffic volume or capacity on congested roads can provide relatively large reductions in traffic delay. Modeling by Deakin and Harvey (1998) indicate that a percentage reduction in urban vehicle mileage tends to produce about twice the percentage reduction in traffic congestion delays.

Analysis by Zupan (2001) indicates that each 1 percent increase in Vehicle Movement Time (VMT) in a U.S. urban region was associated with a 3.5 percent increase in congestion delays in that region during the 1980's, but this relationship disappeared during the 1990s. This change may reflect increased ability of travelers to avoid peak-period driving, through flextime, telework and suburbanization of destinations, allowing VMT growth without comparable increases in congestion delay. The relationship between vehicle travel and congestion delay is probably must stronger when evaluated at a more disaggregated level, for example, on individual corridors or roads.

"Traffic incidents" (disabled vehicles and accidents) account for an estimated 60 percent of delay hours. Although random events, they tend to cause the greatest delays where traffic volumes approach road capacity and so are considered congestion costs. In uncongested conditions an incident causes little or no traffic delay, but a stalled car on the shoulder of a congested road can produce 100-200 vehicle hours of delay on adjacent lanes.

Larger and heavier vehicles tend to require more road space and are slower to accelerate, and so cause more traffic congestion than smaller and lighter vehicles. The relative congestion impact of different vehicles is measured in terms of "Passenger Car Equivalents" or PCEs. Large trucks and buses tend to have 1.5-4 PCEs, depending on roadway conditions and even more through intersections or under stop-and-go driving conditions. A large SUV imposes 1.4 PCEs and a van 1.3 PCEs when traveling through an intersection (Shabih and Kockelman, 1999).

Various indices described in Table 3.1 are used to quantify, monetize (measure in monetary units) and evaluate congestion. These represent different perspectives and assumptions, which can favor one group or set of solutions over others. Some congestion indicators, such as roadway level of service and the Travel Time Index, only consider delays to motorists. Percent Travel Time declines if the total amount of driving on uncongested roads increases, implying that congestion declines if per capita VMT increases, for example, due to increased sprawl. These indicators ignore the benefits to travelers who shift to alternative modes, or from smart growth that increase land use accessibility by clustering common destinations closer together. Indicators that reflect impacts *per capita* rather than *per vehicle* are more suitable for evaluating overall congestion costs.

Table 3.1 : Congestion Indicators

Indicator	Description
Roadway Level Of Service (LOS)	Intensity of congestion delays on a particular roadway or at an intersection, rated from A (uncongested) to F (extremely congested).
Travel Time Rate	The ratio of peak period to free-flow travel times, considering only reoccurring delays (normal congestion delays).
Travel Time Index	The ratio of peak period to free-flow travel times, considering both reoccurring and incident delays (e.g., traffic crashes).
Percent Travel Time In Congestion	Portion of peak-period vehicle or person travel that occurs under congested conditions.
Congested Road Miles	Portion of roadway miles that are congested during peak periods.
Congested Time	Estimate of how long congested "rush hour" conditions exist
Congested Lane Miles	The number of peak-period lane miles that have congested travel.
Annual Hours Of Delay	Hours of extra travel time due to congestion.

Annual Delay Per Capita	Hours of extra travel time divided by area population.
Annual Delay per Road User	Hours of extra travel time divided by the number of peak period road users.
Excess Fuel consumption	Total additional fuel consumption due to congestion.
Fuel Per Capita	Additional fuel consumption divided by area population
Annual Congestion Costs	Hours of extra travel time multiplied times an travel time value, plus the value of additional fuel consumption. This is a monetized congestion cost.
Congestion Cost Per Capita	Additional travel time costs divided by area population
Average Traffic Speed	Average speed of vehicle trips for an area and time (e.g., peak periods).
Average Commute Travel Time	Average commute trip time.
Average Per Capita Travel Time	Average total time devoted to travel.

The table above summarizes various congestion cost indicators. Some only consider impacts on vehicle traffic and ignore the benefits of shifts to alternative modes or reductions in travel distances, and so are unsuited for evaluating the congestion reduction benefits of most TDM strategies.

The first serious method of measuring the amount of congestion and converting it into an economic value, was devised by Glanville and Smeed (1958). They proposed that the calculated total cost of delay depends on what is regarded as a reasonable speed for traffic. Under light traffic conditions on good roads, the average speed of traffic is about 40 km/h in built-up areas, and 65 km/h in non built-up areas. This method however, did not take into account the non-working time. If this was included at the same (high) value as working time, the overall cost will increase manifold. The British Road Federation (1988) made a calculation, using essentially the same method as Glanville and Smeed, and concluded: "The additional cost over and above that experienced in free flow conditions is defined as the congestion cost.

The CBI (1989) describe costs of lost hours of production due to late arrival of staff, vehicle maintenance and repairs, fuel consumption, overtime payments, stock levels, and purchase of additional vehicles. Dodgson and Lane (1997), describe the cost of congestion as the number of vehicles multiplied by the difference between the average generalised cost per vehicle in free-flow conditions and in the actual conditions, and disaggregating for many road types and vehicle types.

The DETR (2000) defined congestion in a way which is closely connected with the earlier studies, but not easily compared with them. Their definition was "average time delay per vehicle-km", defined in turn as "the difference between the actual speed encountered and the free flow speed", but all expressed as an index, or a percentage change on that index.

Congestion is thus an externality imposing macro economic impact on the economy and individuals.

(b) Road Accidents

Road traffic injuries are a global problem affecting all sectors of the society. As World Health

Organization estimates (WHO 2003), in 2000 around 1.26 million people worldwide died as a result of road traffic injuries. Road traffic injuries accounted for 2.2 per cent of global mortality and were responsible for 25 per cent of all deaths due to injury. Around the world, injuries are among the leading cause of death for people aged 15 to 45, and road traffic injuries are responsible for 25 per cent of all deaths due to injury (WHO 2003). Road traffic injuries also exact a heavy toll in terms of the ill health they cause. The ill health, or morbidity, that results from road traffic injuries also differs widely by region, with South-East Asia accounting for more than one third of the morbidity resulting from road traffic injuries each year.

Among the most affected are the pedestrians and motorized two wheelers accounting for 70 to 90 percent of all accidents in the country. Public authorities all over the world are concerned about how to take efficient steps towards lower accident rates on the roads as the volume of motorised traffic and the numbers of accidents have been growing significantly. It is generally believed that improved road conditions and technological improvements in vehicular design result in fall in accident rates. However, as the road users, facing a safer environment, tend to be less careful, the direct effects of the improvements in road safety can be substantially eroded. In economic terms such responses from road users on external safety improvements are called 'moral hazard' (World Bank 1996). Therefore, the safety programs have to keep this aspect in view.

Besides, interventions have to be socially optimal. In addition to the direct investment in safer roads, the public authorities have the opportunity to improve traffic safety by different kinds of interventions, such as orders and prohibitions given by law or by informational and advertising campaigns. The introduction of compulsory seat belts, speed limits on roads regulations governing the manufacturing and safety of automobiles and driving tests are all examples of public authorities intervention. Although direct governmental regulations may not be socially preferred means in securing welfare optimal road safety due to moral hazard effects, they are commonly practiced.

There are four aspects included in the Economics of Road Safety. First, taking the supply side approach, cost of accidents to the society and those affected is analyzed. Second on the demand side willingness of people to pay to avoid or curb accidents is calculated. Third is the macro economic dimension. Macro economic consequences of road accidents and measures to improve safety, are examined. Finally is the dimension of liability arising out of accidents. The prime cause of concern is whom to burden with the liability of damages of the accidents. Should it be the Insurance Companies or the party causing the damage? Increasingly, the polluter pays principle is being adopted to justify full resource cost based user charges word wide. These four dimensions are complementary rather than substitute as each of them applies to different economic issues and prospective. Road safety needs to be addressed at the macro level when policy strategies and legislations are being decided, and at the micro economic level for initiating a specific action.

Estimation of the accident costs is an important aspect of study in transport economics. Accidents costs can be ex post and ex ante. Total *ex post* accident costs are literally incalculable (Jansson 2003). They consist of profound grief and suffering in the cases of death and disability, and various material losses in all cases. The cost of traffic accidents consists of two components. First is the cost of premature loss of life and reduced quality of health. Second is the loss of income and remedial expenditure on medicine and material. The parties paying these costs are the direct victims of the accidents, the relatives and friends, private sector third parties and the public sector. Whereas loss of incomes and remedial expenditures can be estimated based on available statistics, the value of life lost and reduced health quality are usually estimated with the help of willingness studies.

Three components of the *ex ante* accident cost can be distinguished for each particular type of accident, for example, fatalities:

f(r) = willingness to pay for complete safety on the part of the household to which a certain person exposed to the risk of death belongs, as a function of the risk, r. The "value of a statistical life" (VSL) is commonly defined by the derivative of f(r). Assuming for simplicity that f(r) is linear in the relevant range of very low risk values, this relationship can be written = ar.

g(r) = willingness to pay for complete safety on the part of relatives and friends of the person exposed to the risk of death; g(r) br for low values of r.

h(r) = willingness to pay for complete safety on the part of the rest of society; h(r) = cr.

While the value of a fatality risk reduction for households including potential victims of traffic accidents gives rise to the major part of the total value of a statistical life, the components **b** and **c** representing the values of a statistical life to relatives and friends of victims of traffic accidents, and to the rest of society, respectively, are both quite appreciable. The former value is obviously less certain than the latter, corresponding to purely material costs, but from Jones-Lee (1992), Schwab and Soguel (1995), and Lindberg (1999) it can be taken that the value of **b** is substantial (about four-tenths of **a**).

However, reduction in risk of dying as a result of road accident may occur with a time lag. The policy changes, technological improvements and road engineering interventions are likely to take sometime before their effect becomes noticeable. To value the benefits of such policies, it is necessary to ask people how much they would be willing to pay now for reduction of risk that takes place in future. Economic theory suggests that willingness to pay for a future risk reduction should be less than WTP for an immediate risk reduction of the same size. This occurs for two reasons. First, the individual may not be alive to enjoy the risk reduction. This is especially more prominent among the older people. Second, if the individual is willing to substitute consumption for risk (as is usually the case in respect of poor people), the risk reduction should be discounted at the consumption rate of discount. A key question for policy is exactly how much WTP is reduced by a gap between the initiation of a program and time at which the risk reduction is delivered.

Incorporating a value of loss of life and reduced health quality is the recent addition in the transport planning. In terms of macroeconomic impacts of road accidents, it is often suggested that GDP which is most commonly used to measure nation's economic performance should be corrected for loss to the quality of life due to accidents. It is often seen that the conventional measure of GDP does not take into account the adverse changes that take place in quality of life. These corrections have led to the calculation of *"Green GDP"* which allows for loss of environmental capital due to the economic activities. As persistently high levels of traffic accidents require a high level of emergency preparedness in the hospitals, with large number of people waiting for treatment in the hospitals in the developing countries, human and physical capital would be locked in to do much task rather than other tasks that enhance GDP. This implies that the net effect of traffic accidents on GDP is likely to be negative even if conventionally measured and other welfare related aspects of an accident are not measured and monetized such as suffering by victims and their loved ones, or by people waiting in hospital lines due to the extra medical care required by the accident victims.

Given the level of GDP, the total accident costs are higher in countries with high health and system risks. **Health risk** is measured as the annual number of people killed in traffic accidents per 100000 inhabitants; **System risk** is defined as the same numerator per 100000 vehicles. However, statistics on these risks measures could be misleading when comparing countries with varying levels of development. It is seen that the less economically developed a country is the more is the bias towards serious under reporting of accidents and over reporting of vehicle fleet due to non deletion of scrapped vehicles.

In order to understand the share of road accidents in deaths caused in a country or region,it may be useful to find out the place of road accidents among the causes of death in DALY (Disability Adjusted Life Years lost) tables. World Bank (1993) in its publication titled, "World Development Report, Investing in Health" provides a thorough insight into the methodology of calculating DALYs. DALYs express years of life lost to premature death and years lived with a disability, adjusted for the severity of the disability. Disability Adjusted Life Years lost are calculated by combining losses from premature death (defined as the difference between actual age at death and life expectancy at that age in a low-mortality population), and loss of healthy life resulting from disability. Among the 10 important causes of DALYs, road accidents figure in the number two place (Table 3.2).

Table 3.2: Ten Major Causes of DALY in Developing Countries (1990)

Sr.	*Disease or Injury*	*Percentage of total*
1.	Unpopular Major Depression	7.0
2.	Road Traffic Accidents	6.3
3.	Tuberculosis	6.0
4.	Violence	5.5
5.	Alcohol use	4.7
6.	War	4.1
7.	Bipolar disorder	3.1
8.	Self-inflicted injuries	3.0
9.	Schizophrenia	2.8
10.	Iron deficiency anemia	2.7

Source: Murray and Lopez (1996)

Finally is the issue of compensating the victims for losses due to accidents. This particular aspect is covered under law of torts. Under the law of torts damage compensation can be claimed only if harm has been done. A second element is causation. The injurer must be cause-in-fact and a proximate cause of harm, if he is to be held liable for the loss. The cases of motor accidents constitute the major bulk of tort cases in India. Rules regarding damage payments by injurers to victims are called liability rules. A liability rule typically specifies as to how much payment is to be made by the injurer to the victim. For instance the rule of negligence holds him liable only if he was negligent no matter the level of care taken by the victim. The rule of negligence with the defence of contributory negligence hold injurer liable only if he was negligent and the victim was not. In India, the rule requires proportional sharing of liability when both parties are negligent.

Economic analysis deals with the important question of whether and how much damage payments are to be made by the injurer to the victim. The measure of damage can be considered in two respects. First, is its ability to influence the incentive for the injurer to take optimal care. In case of total burden shifted to the injurer, the injurer will take full possible care. Second, it determines who should bear the risk of an accident. For efficiency considerations, it is argued (Arlen 2000) that damage compensation should be exactly equal to the harm. It has been shown that when compensation is equal to the damage, the injurer will take efficient care. In economic analysis, inefficient behavior is considered as the cause of the harm and hence a reason for invoking the liability. It has been considered that for a liability rule to be efficient, it is necessary that the injurer is made to internalize the cost of entire externality created by them.

(c) Environmental Effects

For many poor people in developing countries, the inability to access jobs, education, and health facilities is viewed as the most serious constraint on their quality of life. Motorized transport is often crucial to poor people, but because they frequently live and work in the shadow of motorized transport, they are also the most vulnerable to its adverse environmental impacts. Environmental protection must therefore be seen as an essential part of the task of improving the quality of life of the poor, and not as a luxury to be purchased at the expense of the poor's mobility. A comprehensive strategy for transport and the urban environment should cover the built environment, including land take, urban form, visual intrusion of infrastructure and traffic, and cultural heritage; the social effects of transport in causing occupational or locational resettlement and community severance; personal safety and security; and the more commonly recognized problems of noise and air pollution (local, regional, and global). All of these concerns must be formally addressed in a typical project's environmental assessment.

In developing countries an estimated 0.5 million to 1 million people die prematurely each year as a result of respiratory and other illnesses caused by exposure to urban air pollution. This is a larger number than those dying as a consequence of urban traffic accidents, although because of the age distribution of those afflicted, traffic accidents probably reduce life-years more. Exposure to lead contributes to behavioral problems and learning disabilities in urban children. It also reduces the quality of life.

Road transport contributes significantly to urban air pollution in many countries. The World Health Organization estimates that suspended particulate matter leads to the premature death of over 0.5 million people per year. The economic costs of air pollution have been estimated to be equivalent to about 2 percent of Gross Domestic Product in many countries. Incorporation of environmental issues within an urban transport strategy requires the identification of the main transport-generated pollutants (usually suspended particulate matter, lead, and ozone) and the mobilization of technical, fiscal, and system management controls on fuel and vehicle technology to reduce these pollutants. Frequently these will also contribute to a desirable reduction of greenhouse gas emissions.

A "business-as-usual" scenario for the transport sector offers little prospect of relief. The principal components determining the level of GHG emissions in transport are the level of activity (in ton or passenger kilometers), the modes of transport used, the energy intensity of each mode, and the mix of fuels used. In the industrialized countries, transport activity has increased alongside the economic growth, the shift to the private car and air transport has worsened the modal balance effect, and changes in the balance of fuels has had little impact. It is only the dramatic increase in fuel efficiency that has acted as a brake on GHG emissions. Even so, transport GHG emissions continue to grow in the industrialized countries even though overall emissions have been stabilized. Economic growth in the developing countries similarly threatens to dominate any attenuating effect of technology improvement. To avert this outcome requires a combination of transportation policy reforms in the short term and technological changes in the longer term.

Fossil fuel consumption is influenced directly by fuel choice, vehicle size, and fuel efficiency, and indirectly by individual and corporate decisions on activity location and style, and transport mode. Emissions of methane come largely from leakages of gasoline, diesel, and unburned natural gas and are thus susceptible to influence by fueling infrastructure improvement. The strongest incentive to fuel economy in actions in all these dimensions is the monetary cost of fuel. It has been shown that pollution controls supported by appropriate prices or taxes are much more effective than is the use of regulations alone. The current generation of diesel vehicles appears to be more damaging to public health than is gasoline or gas-powered vehicles. Thus, while diesel is a particularly efficient fuel from the point of view of reducing GHG emissions, only the new generation of clean diesels should have a role in GHG strategy. Furthermore, mitigation measures for local pollution focus on emissions of vehicles in use, whereas the entire life cycle (from well to tailpipe) is relevant for analysis of GHG emissions.

Mobile sources, particularly motor vehicles, are a major cause of air pollution. Motor vehicles emit CO, HCs, NOx, SO_2, and other toxic substances such as TSP and Pb. Emission rates of CO and HCs from diesel vehicles are lower than that of gasoline vehicles because of better combustion efficiencies. While the emission rate of NOx is higher in diesel vehicles because of lower combustion temperatures, diesel vehicles emit TSP and higher levels of SO_2 but not Pb. The growing vehicle population is a major contributor to air pollution problems. Initially, these problems were most apparent in city centres but over the last two decades lakes and streams and even remote forests have experienced significant degradation. As evidence of anthropogenic impacts on the upper atmosphere accumulates, there is increasing concern about the part played by motor vehicles in global warming.

Motor vehicles constitute the main source of air pollution in most of the cities in the developing countries. This is particularly true of the CO, NOx, and to a lesser extent, SPM, HCs, SO_2 emissions into the atmosphere. Four factors make pollution from vehicles more serious in developing countries. First, many vehicles are in poor condition, creating more particulates and burning fuels inefficiently. Certain types of engines, such as two strokes, are particularly bad. The two stroke engines emit hydrocarbons and smoke up to 10 times the rate of modern four stroke engines and produce the vast majority of the emissions. Second, lower quality of fuels are used, leading to the emissions of far greater quantities of CO_2 emissions in a rapidly changing world scenario pollutants. Third, motor vehicles are concentrated in a few large cities. Fourth, a far larger percentage of the population moves and lives in the open, and is thus exposed to automotive pollutants.

A comprehensive assessment of the nature and magnitude of transport-induced air pollution in developing countries is precluded by the complexity of the contributory factors and lack of reliable information. However, studies reveal that:

- the contribution of transport to air pollution in developing countries will increase substantially with the growth in motorization; and

- transport air pollution in developing countries is largely an urban phenomenon confined mainly to very large cities with a high proportion of trips by buses, automobiles, motorcycles, and other two- and three-wheeled vehicles.

3.4 Conclusion

The external impacts such as congestion, environmental impacts and accident costs have recently been the focus of much of transport research in India and abroad. Transport planning gains significance to increase the economic impacts and reduce externalities. To effectively reduce transport externalities, it is important to change transport pricing so that they are a better reflection of the marginal social cost of transport. Since transport demand is expected to grow further, the need for a better transport pricing will only be increased in future. It is argued (Frey et.al 1985) that the support for the transport pricing is the strongest in the academy and got progressively weaker the closer one got to the trenches where the policies were actually made. Therefore, it is often felt that due to political and technological reasons it is likely that the reform process in the transport pricing will only be implemented gradually.

4

POLICY INSTRUMENTS AND TRANSPORT EXTERNALITIES

4.1 Introduction

As the root cause of the transport externalities is the fact that the damage constitutes external costs that do not appear in the utility functions of those who cause such damage, there is a need to internalize these costs in order to persuade those responsible to give consideration to the impact of their acts on the society at large. The policy mix of major instruments available for tackling transport problems can be classified into four broad groups: using markets, creating markets, using legislative powers, and engaging the public.

Discussions in this chapter focus on the instruments used worldwide to mitigate the external impacts of transport. Starting with market based instruments, the command and control instruments and the instruments making use of the public opinion are discussed. In the end it is concluded that it is not possible to control the externalities by any one instrument, instead, a mix of all instruments has to be applied to achieve optimal results.

4.2 Using the Markets

There are two distinct advantages of market based instruments. First, although they appear to be little blunter than others, market based instruments are often easier to implement. Second, the market based instruments have important fiscal considerations in terms of raising revenue through user charges. As the basic source of externalities is that pricing system is not applied in public goods, pricing the public goods is one of the alternatives offered by the economists (Baumol and Oates, 1988; Jeanrenaud, 1997). Using markets therefore involves moving towards free market prices on the one hand (by levying user charges) and moving beyond free market prices (by providing subsidies) on the other hand. The instruments applied for this purpose are also called incentive based, as the sole purpose of the instruments is to modify the behaviour of the polluters. All of these have one characteristic in common: they make the polluters aware of opportunity cost of the resources and lead to the internalization of damage. These instruments are also called the economic instruments. The primary characteristics of these are:

- The instruments aim at modifying the behaviour of the polluters by persuading them to take account of the damage for which they are responsible;
- The behaviour modification is based on incentives rather than constraints;
- The polluter is informed of the cost of utilizing environmental resources either directly (charge) or indirectly (market); and
- The polluter is free to choose the most suitable means of reducing emissions.

Among the most important economic instruments are: taxes/charges, subsidies, and tradable permits.

4.2.1 Taxes

Taxes can be used as policy instruments to correct the problem of over-pricing or under-pricing of the resources characterized with public good nature. One basic difference between the direct controls and the pricing techniques is the way they treat the environmentally damaging activities. While the former consider them as illegal, the latter reckon them as a part of the economic activity that should certainly be curtailed, but not with the use of the police powers of the state. The fiscal approach uses the meter rather than the police inspector for enforcement. For instance, tax on leaded gasoline requires no more than the record of the quantity sold. Taxing the polluters for the privilege of polluting certainly affects their economic behaviour. Tax assumes the role of a cost, which has to be internalized. Among the major applications of taxation policy in the transport sector are:

(a) Parking charges

The act of parking is a close complement of vehicle use, especially in the case of urban transport. Charging a toll for parking may be needed to cover the cost of the parking space, and to allocate existing space efficiently. From the transport economics standpoint, the idea is to discourage vehicle use by taxing a close complement. The outcome could be a lower level of mobility. As a measure of restraint, parking charges are considered to be less sophisticated and hence more suitable for developing countries. Their effectiveness essentially depends on level and their structure. Among the alternate forms in which these are generally prevalent are fixed lump sum, constant hourly charges, a two part tariff and variable hourly charges. While the fixed lump sum, constant hourly or fixed hourly charges are not very effective against congestion; the variable hourly charges are often used to tackle congestion. The charges are kept at different levels during the day and are at the highest level during the peak hours in the morning as well as in the evening. Rates of parking fees often vary between on street and off street parking with on street being the costlier and normally based on variable hourly charges.

Among the main weaknesses of this policy is the fact that it penalizes 'stopping' traffic vs. 'through' traffic and shorter trips vs. longer ones. Probability of higher parking charges in the cities generating more trips and hence congestion are always higher which has the potential of rendering parking as an anti congestion measure ineffective. Even more importantly, it leaves open the problem of regulating privately owned parking facilities.

(b) Vehicle License Fees

This constitutes a way of increasing the fixed costs of vehicle use. The often used measure is to increase the import duty, sales tax on vehicles or vehicle license fees. Among the potential disadvantages of high import duty structure are they result in local population being discouraged to use better technology imported vehicles which are often more fuel efficient, safe and less polluting. Besides, they tend to encourage people to use vehicles for a longer time which may result in older vehicles being in operation. The license fees are also not very effective in reducing vehicle ownership as these often become a part of vehicle cost and unless used in a very dynamic tax structure, their real values get lower with inflation. It is not suitable to take into account when and where the vehicle is used and the external costs of congestion are higher. For the same reason, it might be less powerful compared to policies that increase the marginal costs of mobility.

(c) Fuel Tax as a Surrogate User Price

Fuel tax is also another tool to increase the operating costs of vehicles. There is a natural correlation between road congestion and fuel use. Higher congestion means lower speed and longer waiting times, implying higher fuel consumption. Taxing fuel has the effect of raising the marginal private cost of mobility. It is usually the only cost that is incurred directly in making a trip. It therefore has a potential of affecting the choice of travel mode, number of trips, choice of vehicle technology and to an extent trade off between the travel cost and the location of dwelling and work. It is generally recommended that (World Bank 2002) the price of fuel should reflect the true resource cost.

The importance of taxing fuels at a level that reflects the externalities, as well as the border costs and any proxy charges for road maintenance costs, is often emphasized although the cost of mitigating impacts is logically a better foundation for defining appropriate levels of environmental taxation. Around the world the retail price of diesel is typically lower than that of gasoline, because of differential taxation. The trend is particularly pronounced in South Asia. In India, for example, the retail price of gasoline was almost double the price of diesel. A large price differential between kerosene and gasoline, based on the use of kerosene by the poor as a domestic heating fuel, leads to illegal addition of kerosene to gasoline, resulting in higher pollutant emissions.

Hence it is necessary to develop tax structures that protect the urban environment but that do not discourage use of the most economical fuel by agriculture or intercity freight vehicles. One possible way of doing that is to identify the most damaging vehicle types (cars, urban mini-buses, and vans) and use high duties on those types of diesel vehicle, rather than fuel taxation, as the means of changing the balance of economic advantage. That is already being done in some countries by exempting clean vehicles from import duties or vehicle license duties. Another option is to increase the tax on diesel to make the price of automotive diesel comparable to that of gasoline, but to rebate industrial and agricultural users of diesel. This approach has been adopted successfully in Chile. Another is to tax automotive diesel more and use a dye to distinguish automotive diesel from diesel for other uses.

As a measure of road maintenance charge, fuel tax does not differentiate well by vehicle type, and often needs to be supplemented by the axle weight charging to discourage over load. As a congestion charge also it fails to reflect the structure of congestion well in any area as it can not be differentiated area wise. As an environmental cess also it fails to be very useful as it fails to promote less emitting technology. Besides, it has certain administrative difficulties also in implementation. These essentially emanate from the problem of multiple uses in which a particular fuel could be put to. For example diesel is used for transportation of goods and kerosene is used as domestic fuel for cooking. Nevertheless, fuel tax has a distinct advantage over the ownership fees as it is directly related to the vehicle use.

There are therefore some limitations of use of tax as an instrument of control. First, one significant weakness of the tax approach, is uncertainty about the magnitude of its effects. It is difficult to ascertain as to how much increase in tax will bring how much decrease in externalities. It is therefore argued that the tax as an instrument of control of pollution in areas characterized by threshold effect, cannot be effective. Second, it is argued that it poses unnecessary burden and promote distortions. Finally, environmentalist object to the levy of the tax as it gives license to the polluters to pollute.

4.2.2 Subsidies

There are basically two types of subsidies: unit subsidies and grants to defray the cost of pollution control equipment. The unit subsidies are payments based on reduction in discharges. The grants on the other hand are payments made to offset the cost of pollution control equipment. The use of subsidies to prevent pollution is to use carrot rather than the stick. Though the use of tax or subsidies may appear to be similar, the tax approach has been held to be superior to the subsidy approach for two reasons (Baumol and Oats 1988). First, effluent taxes clearly reduce the profitability of firms by imposing an extra cost on them. Subsidies, on the other hand, increase the profitability of the firms and may allow the most polluting firm to be in business. Moreover, these make the industry more profitable thus allowing the entry of more polluting firms into the business. Second, there are administrative problems of distributing the subsidies. The environment authority has to lay down certain benchmarks for release of subsidies and there are problems in fixing benchmarks. Potential applications in transport include subsidies on purchase of models with less emissions and energy saving and subsidizing substitutes to privately owned vehicles, such as the public transport.

Public transport subsidies are a form of positive restraints which can encourage use of public transport by the car owners. It is seen that its elasticities are higher in off peak travel when travel is more for leisure and optional (World Bank 2002). However, the biggest limitation with subsidies is that they promote irresponsible behavior, remove incentives to reduce cost and thus promote tendency towards more and more subsidies.

4.3 Creating the Markets

Market creation is another important way to reduce the externalities. Defining property rights, privatizing, and establishing tradable permits and rights are all examples of innovations underway for market creation.

4.3.1 Allocation of Property Rights

An alternate approach to solving the problems of pollution and congestion attempts to attack the root cause of the problem: the problem of the ownership of the resources. As the resources in common pool do not belong to any individual and hence are over-exploited. The society's resources are often in greater danger if these are held as common property. Anyone who decides to exploit them suffers a very small fraction of loss. The advocates of this approach believe that redefining the property rights can solve the problem. It is argued that in an economy with well-defined and transferable property rights, individuals and firms have every incentive to use resources as efficiently as possible. The theory derives support from 'Coase theorem' (Coase, 1960). According to Coase, given certain assumptions, the most efficient solution to pollution damage situations is a bargaining process between polluter and the sufferer. Each could compensate other according to who possesses property rights. If the polluter has the right, the sufferer can compensate him for not polluting, alternatively, if the sufferer has the right, the polluter can compensate him to tolerate the damage.

One way of solving the problem of congestion on roads is to define the property rights and limit the access to roads. The permits to drive are issues on the bases of willingness to pay and the permits are tradable so that drivers with higher marginal benefits would be willing to buy the rights to enter the restricted areas and individuals with very low marginal benefits would be willing to sell such rights. It amounts to creating the markets for driving permits to restricted areas. The trade would eventually end equalizing the marginal cost of driving across road users and social welfare would be maximized.

4.3.2 Privatization

Privatization of the infrastructure could be another option of market creation. Privatization of road infrastructure and public transport services could be resorted to facilitate internalization of costs and full realization of costs of operations through the private investors.

4.3.3. Tradable Permits

Tradable permits are second major category of market based instruments. As opposed to acting directly on prices, as it is done in case of charges or taxes, the government fixes the maximum quantity of emissions by companies by giving a corresponding amount of permits. Each permit entitles the firm to emit a particular level of pollutants. Companies, however, have the option of buying and selling permits or even holding on them for future use. The market forces: demand and supply, determine the price of the permit. As long as the price of the permit is lower than the marginal cost of abatement, the company prefers to buy them in comparison to purchase of technologies to combat pollution.

One important example of application of this instrument is the case of Singapore. As the trend increase of vehicles was excessive in Singapore and the tax as an instrument to control vehicle ownership was not proving to be very effective, the Singapore government introduced a scheme of Vehicle Quota System (VQS) in 1991. VQS is now a principle tool of control of vehicle ownership in Singapore. Under the scheme, the government announces the maximum number of vehicles, by vehicle type, that could be registered in the country. In accordance with the quota determined, the certificates are auctioned in an open bidding process. The VQS addresses the issues of equity by structuring the bid prices in accordance with the vehicle type and capacity.

The marketable permits can do a better job than tax in four respects. First, their receipts are unaffected by inflation. With the rising prices and declining real value of the currency, the bid will automatically rise to maintain the real earnings. Second, with rise in number of units and permits remaining unchanged, the prices of permits increase leading to a tendency to outbid the existing holders or incentive to reduce the emission. Third, it is possible to keep the levels of pollution and congestion in accordance with the sensitivity of the area or locality. For more fragile areas, smaller number of vehicle permits can be allotted.

4.4 Using Legislative Powers

Also known as the Command-And-Control (CAC) strategy, the direct controls consist of measures aimed at influencing the behavior of agents causing damage directly and continue to play a leading role in developing countries where incentive-based strategies are being introduced. There is a wide range of available instruments: emission standards, permits, zoning and bans. However, these can be classified into two broad categories namely (a) emission standards, which limit the quantities or concentration of pollutants, which may be emitted, (b) restrictions concerning the use of specific equipment or procedures. Usually, ensuring the emission levels at the pre-fixed standards is rather difficult job. It is often done with the help of metering devices, which is complex and error prone. Therefore, the second type of direct controls is more effective. Prescribing a technology offers an advantage of avoiding actual monitoring of emissions because it is possible to ensure that it has been actually used. The most common examples of such controls in the transport sector are prescribing Euro II norms for vehicles, complete bans on use of non-CNG vehicles in a particular area, banning use of two stroke engines in two and three wheelers, and providing safety standards to be adhered to by the manufacturers.

The limits of this approach appear when the emphasis is placed on the cost-effectiveness of policies. Simplicity is obtained at the cost of flexibility, since the polluter is no longer in a position to choose the abatement technology it feels is most appropriate and least expensive. This is notwithstanding the fact that the polluter may be more familiar with abatement technologies than the regulatory agencies. Moreover, in view of the changing technologies, banning a facility or a procedure rapidly becomes a source of criticism.

Apart from the technology based mandates, the command and control measures in case of transport are classified into two categories. First, are the controls relating to the vehicle technology and upkeep and maintenance of vehicles. These essentially flow from the motor legislations like act and rules. Second kind of controls typically relate to the vehicles usage. These are in the form of parking restrictions, congestion related entry restrictions and ownership restrictions in the form of quotas. The vehicle technology related controls generally aim at pollution reduction and safety considerations.

In India, the standards of motor vehicle production, usage and maintenance are sought to be implemented through the provisions of the Central Motor Vehicles Rules, 1989. The rules have been made under the Motor Vehicles Act, 1988. The rules lay down emission and safety standards for motor vehicles in India. The standards have been set for the durability of catalytic converters, particulate emission by the diesel vehicles, and carbon and hydro carbon emission by the petrol vehicles. The Ministry of Environment and Forest Government of India has also prescribed the fuel standards for India under the Environment Protection Act.

To apply environmental standards, it will be necessary to design appropriate vehicle inspection and maintenance programs, scrappage programs, as well as ensure that related policies are appropriate, and provide the correct incentives, including those related to domestic taxation, trade liberalization, and public expenditures.

Vehicle emissions standards and technologies are not effective without proper maintenance. Poorly maintained vehicles are high emitters and are responsible for a disproportionate share of total vehicle emissions. Wider use of spot-checking equipment capable of identifying major problems from any relevant vehicle type, and of fixed I/M stations for more thorough examination and follow-up of vehicles so identified, holds promise of significant impact on the pollution problem. An appropriate system of fines, and controls thereof, could also make such system self-financing. World Bank (2002) suggests that an I/M system based on centralized, high-volume, inspection-only centers with computerized emissions measurement to minimize tampering and corruption, is likely to be more effective than is a decentralized system with a large number of private garages participating in the I/M. If the proper controls are in place, the private sector can be an important partner in operating effective I/M programs.

When emissions standards are enforced effectively, the cost of owning old vehicles actually increases, making vehicle renewal more attractive. Vehicle retirement and scrappage programs can further encourage this phenomenon as long as it is possible to identify gross emitters that are operating at a high annual rate of vehicle kilometers and that still have reasonable remaining economic lives. However, considerable care is needed in designing such schemes as using age as a proxy for high emissions may not always identify the worst cases. If the program is directed at urban pollution, it must also prevent the import of old vehicles from outside the city to take advantage of the retirement bonus. As is often seen in the developing countries that in the absence of maximum lifespan of vehicles, gross emitters are mostly owned by low-income households that are often in no position to purchase much newer vehicles. Cash-for-scrappage schemes may be more effective than cash-for-replacement schemes. In the most polluted areas, it may even be possible to use cash-for-scrappage schemes to influence modal split. In many developing countries, commercial vehicles (buses, trucks, and taxis) are the greatest contributors to urban air pollution. Some countries have been quite successful in stimulating early replacement of these vehicles.

The parking behavior can be controlled by limiting the total stock of parking spaces, by regulating the parking spaces in terms of location, purpose, duration and timings. The parking spaces could be public ally managed and privately managed. While it is easier to handle public parking spaces, it may be difficult to regulate the private parking places especially the ones which are located in the down town areas. As is mostly seen, if located in the heart of the city, such places often induce the car owners to drive to the down town areas thereby aggravating the problem of congestion. Regulations have therefore to take into account their contribution to traffic generation and flow. Parking strategies in the form of park and ride or kiss and ride can be very helpful though it may add to the problem of pollution in the areas where they are located.

Likewise, area bans can be designed with or without exemptions. These could be in the form of local area bans such as pedestrian streets. In certain cases some areas could be declared as the car free zones. However, area ban measures with some kind of preferred vehicles status can be categorized as permit based and time allocation systems. Often the difficulty with the permit based systems is their amenability to criticism to the way permits are allocated and their potential in encouraging rent seeking behavior. Time allocation is another option often used to control congestion. Under the system, allocation of travel time is made on certain predetermined formula like odd and even system. The system permits only vehicles with odd numbers on their license plates to enter the restricted area on odd dates and vehicles with even numbers on even dates. However, this system is often criticized for its inability to take care of the user need and that it does not necessarily reduce congestion as it may promote scarcity psyche resulting in people making additional trips on the day they are allowed to ply vehicles.

4.5 Engaging the Public

The final set of instruments involves public in preventing damage to the resources. It is often seen that the governments respond more effectively to the public demand than tackling the problem on their own. Consequently information disclosures and educating the public are the two major tools using the public to tackle the problems of externalities.

4.5.1 Information Disclosures

The information disclosures require the firms producing a specific good or using a potentially hazardous good to make disclosures on the technology used or the environmental effects of its operation or the final product. For example the firms are made to specify the details of emission from the motor vehicles, the abatement technology applied on a particular model (for example Euro II or Euro III compliant technology) and the emissions levels of each models. The public is then in a position to make choice among the models available. The information disclosures could also allow the public to monitor the performance of the models, create pressure against the polluting models (for example the two stroke versus four stroke autos) and demanding incentives for promotion of less polluting technologies (for example CNG).

4.5.2 Educating the Public

It involves educating and informing individuals to make them aware of the consequences of their actions on the well being of the population or the future generations (for example, emissions by ill maintained vehicles, problems of disposal of motor vehicle waste, and risks of driving without a helmet or drunken driving). It is very effective tool in case of activities with potential of mass scale violations. Mostly intensive education campaigns are launched to educate the people about the growing transport problems. The campaigns seek their support for the initiatives like greater use of public transport and non-motorized modes, proper maintenance of vehicles, replacement of very old vehicles and safer driving practices.

Generally speaking, moral suasion can be successful in following three situations:

(i) Where the fiscal measures like taxes and subsidies fail to generate enough funds for the maintenance of environmental quality. Such a situation forces a very low allocation of funds for the basic necessities in the public utility services forcing the environmental protection to be relegated to the background. This is typically the case in the developing countries.

(ii) It can also be helpful in situations where the polluters are not identified so that they can be subjected to other direct control measures like taxes and subsidies,

(iii) The measure may also be very useful in the situation of sudden and unexpected episodes of pollution.

One of the most common applications of this measure is in prevention of road accidents. Incomplete information about the risks of driving without appropriate safety equipments leads to behaviour the drivers would not otherwise choose. Poorly informed drivers often underestimate the risk of their actions. Among the propaganda resorted to usually is to reduce deaths and accidents by inexpensive means such as wearing helmets and seat belts, and refraining from driving when intoxicated. However, these measures require repeated individual compliance. Some people comply readily with the required preventive actions producing a very low initial cost, while others are impervious to safety propaganda and can be reached only by repeated multi-pronged propaganda followed by much more expensive measures such as saturating the roads with police to enforce the law.

However, the suasive programmes are not the main stay of the transport regulations, which rely mostly on direct regulation and economic instruments. The success of these programmes to control pollution and improve safety is to a great extent influenced by the strength of the population willing to participate in the voluntary programmes. Hence, where problem of pollution is very high and substantial improvement in environmental quality is posing a problem; direct controls and price incentives are effective.

4.6 Conclusion

The initial analyses in the transport economics literature of optimal pricing of transport were conducted in the first best framework (Mayeres 2003) assuming that the gov.ernments can make use of non-distortionary taxes (a tax is non-distortionary if individuals can do nothing to change the tax) for raising its revenue and achieving its distributional objectives. The first best market solution in the presence of externality could be traced back to Pigou (1920) according to whom an efficient allocation of resources can be obtained by setting the price of a good for consumption or production according to the marginal costs incurred by the society. This way the generator of an externality is faced with a damage that he inflicts to the society. In the case of transport users it will imply making each one of them face the marginal social costs of their trips. It will be necessary to levy a toll equal to the difference between the marginal social cost and the average cost that is already borne by the user. It in turn requires a differentiated toll which varies according to vehicles type, timing, location of travel and other travel characteristics. However, developing such a tax is not practically possible for want of information. Therefore, the second best taxes have to be resorted to.

Tax structures that discourage the purchase of new vehicles—for example, registration fees or excise taxes based on the market value of the vehicle—may have adverse environmental impacts that should be weighed against their perceived distribution effects. Possible measures include replacing import tariffs on new vehicles by ownership taxes reflecting the environmental quality of the vehicle, eliminating the system under which vehicle registration fees are proportional to the book value of the vehicle (which makes it more expensive to own new vehicles than old ones), and minimizing the tax on the purchase of new vehicles. The fiscal impact of these changes might need to be offset by an increase in direct charges for road use. In some middle-income countries, it may be necessary to consider a safety net to offset the immediate impact of making it more costly for the poor to operate old vehicles, particularly in the taxi trade.

Setting relative tax levels is a complex issue. In principle, one should identify the emissions values of different pollutants and structure vehicle and fuel taxes to reflect differences in the summed value of emissions for different vehicle types. In practice, however, emissions levels depend not only on the fuel type and composition but also on where and how it is burned. Moreover, the evidence on the health costs of different pollutants remains sketchy. At best, then, the use of fiscal incentives would be somewhat rough and ready.

Just as externalities are not the result of a single action, there cannot be a single instrument based solution for the problems caused by them. The process often involves making trade offs. The solution is rarely the first best, but is often in the more realistic world of second best solutions. A useful aspect of the policy mix is that it juxtaposes a wide variety of policy instruments. The policy makers have a range of instruments to choose from after weighing the pros and cons of each one of them. From the experience of different countries in use of policy instruments in tackling the transport externalities it can be concluded that it is important for the policy to fulfill four objectives: achieving financial sustainability, ensuring administrative sustainability, building constituency for change, and achieving policy integration.

5

MOBILISING RESOURCES FROM THE POSITIVE EXTERNALITIES

(Issues in Road Policy)

5.1 Introduction

New roads lower costs of goods and services, facilitate the development of new areas, create new job opportunities and allow the development of urban areas. Due to increases in household car ownership rates, demographic changes and changes in geographical pattern of housing, work and leisure activities; the road networks all over are getting increasingly congested. This entails not only time losses to private and business transport, but also severe noise and environmental pollution and degradation of quality of life. During the past few years, major road capacity expansion schemes have been carried out to improve connectivity and ease congestion. However, road transport is still rapidly increasing and the congestion is getting back in most of the places especially in urban areas. Most transport (be it public or private, passenger or freight, and motorized or non motorized) uses the road system. The effects that a given investment on roads can have on economic activity are manifold. These may vary in terms of geographical and economic area and the actors involved.

The dichotomy highlighted in differences between the Classical and Keynesian models with regard to macro economic impacts of fiscal policy led to division of public expenditure in the form of public consumption spending versus the public investment. While the earlier has the effect of crowding out the private investment hence is unproductive, the latter is often associated with crowding in of private investment thus working as a catalytic agent for development. The first analysis of possible relationship between infrastructure investment and economic growth dates back to the work of Arrow and Kurz (1970). Improvements were later made through the endogenous growth models of Barrow (1993) and Aschauer (1989 and 1993). While Barrow found the negative impacts, Aschauer (1993) showed that the results varied drastically depending on whether the analysis focused on the total spending or spending in infrastructure. The current consensus of research in the area is that the public spending in general has a negative effect on growth while the expenditure on road infrastructure is found to have a positive influence.

One of the often recommended solutions to the problem of road management is road pricing (World Bank 2002). However, it is difficult to find acceptance to the idea and even more difficult to actually implement them in practice. Road pricing is, among other things, a form of taxation. Generally, taxes create inefficient allocations in the economy because they drive a wedge between the marginal cost of production and the price the consumer has to pay. The seriousness of this problem differs however between the different kinds of taxes. Too little is known about how transport taxes perform in this respect. Road pricing strategies inevitably produce a large revenue for the government. The social value of this effect depends on the following factors: distortionary effects of the road pricing in the economy outside of the transport sector; and the way the revenue is used. The effect is less ditortionary if the revenue is used to cut back the most distortionary forms of taxation (like the tax on labour) or to provide a public good for which there is a high willingness-to-pay, or for other purposes than to improve the efficiency of the economy. However, if it is used for funding unproductive expenditures of the government it is likely to minimize social welfare.

It is often argued (World Bank 2002) that it is possible to identify optimal road pricing strategies with the use of a fairly standard transport model and an appropriate optimisation technique, and to study the efficiency gains and distributional issues arising from these strategies by way of cost benefit analysis and a spatial equity analysis. While for ensuring equity considerations, two different techniques are used to optimise the social efficiency objective function (World Bank 2002). They correspond to the cases of "first-best" and "second-best" pricing respectively. In first-best road pricing, all links in the road network can be charged. In second-best road pricing, only a few of the links in the network can be charged.

Discussions in this chapter highlight issues in road management and pricing. Alternative approaches to road pricing are discussed and it is concluded that introducing road pricing is necessary to fund road construction and maintenance.

5.2 Concerns and Options

Among the major concerns that a Road Policy should address are:

(a) Road Construction and Maintenance;

(b) Traffic management to improve traffic system capacity, quality, or safety;

(c) Demand management to secure maximum social value for network use;

(d) Infrastructure expansion planning and appraisal.

(a) Road Construction and Maintenance

In terms of road financing, there are two different approaches followed in the world. The first is the traditional approach. Followed mostly in the developing countries, this approach dwells on the premise that road is a public good to be financed totally through the public expenditure. No attempt is usually made at direct road pricing from the users though in some cases revenues are sought to be generated through the vehicle taxes and fuel taxes. The alternate approach known as the commercial approach treats road as a capital asset so as to apply the principles of commercial accounting to charge the users on cost recovery basis for their road use. The taxes in the sector are designed to minimize the distortions to transport pattern and choices. Road finance remains divorced from the general revenues and the road users exercise their say in the road management.

Funding the maintenance of road is of prime concern. Efforts have to be made to develop mechanism to tap the user based second-generation road funds financed through fuel duty charges or other such user based charges. The proceeds of the same should be spent on the maintenance of roads. The idea of second-generation road fund is based on the dictum that the road infrastructure should be maintained with funds collected from users. It is believed (World Bank 2002) that normally direct and indirect charges to the users should be enough to cover the full costs of traffic including environmental impact and road maintenance. As the road damage caused by the vehicles depends on the vehicle weight per axle, introduction of a kilometer charge that is a function of the number of equivalent standard axle loads of a heavy vehicle is efficient in reducing this type of externality. A tax that is closely linked to the road damage caused by vehicles would give truckers an incentive to reduce axle weights (Small 1992). Fuel taxes are less appropriate for this purpose since that give perverse incentive as the fuel consumption increases with the number of axles.

(b) Traffic Management

The objective of traffic management is to make the safest and most productive use of existing transport system (road based) resources. It seeks to adjust, adapt, manage and improve the existing transport system to meet the specified objective. By maximizing the efficiency, capital expenditure can be avoided. Many traffic management systems like traffic signals increase the efficiency of movement with negligible side effects. However, the traffic management policy involves choices: pedestrian and non-motorized traffic versus motorized traffic. Given the limited road space, both may have conflicting interests. For instance, priority to pedestrians may imply reduced road capacity for the vehicles. An integrated traffic management system will require compromises between competing interests of various users.

The traffic management measures that are useful are roadside parking management, traffic circulation measures, bus service priority and regulatory measures under the Motor Vehicles Act. To prevent roadside parking of vehicles, it is essential that special parking areas are developed. The basic cause of lack of parking facilities in India is that it is presumed that parking has to be provided at a social cost without any additional charge to the users. However, the biggest limitation with this assumption is that often funds are not available from the public resources to provide this facility since no bank loan would be available for a venture with no returns. To facilitate parking areas to come up, it may be appropriate to treat parking space as a normal commodity such as gas or electricity, and to follow the implications of a commercial or market approach for prices and investment policy. Basic principles enunciated by Roth (1965) on parking space allocation are still relevant:

- That existing parking space in towns should be made available to people with most need of it, and

- That since space in towns is scarce, the demand for it must compete with the demand for other land uses (space should be allocated to car parking only if the car parkers need it more than the other users).

Providing a special priority to bus services in the road usage has twin benefits: it reduces road congestion and helps the poor. It is argued (World Bank 2002) that at peak loading, a bus can carry 30 times as many passengers as a car, in only three times the road space. As it is used more by the poor, it facilitates travel by the poor.

Traffic management can however not be seen as a one-shot measure. It has to be a continuous process to ensure that the benefits of congestion reduction achieved by any such intervention are not overtaken by the increasing population of vehicles. Emphasis has to be on creating a favorable institutional environment that encourages effective operation and development of technical skills to implement new techniques.

(c) Demand Management

The economic rationale of demand management is that if the price directly incurred by travelers in making journeys is lower than the full cost of the journey, then some trips will impose a net cost to the community. The full cost of a trip includes personal cost borne by the traveler and the social costs imposed by the traveler on the community in the form of contribution to congestion, the increase in accident potential, and the polluting effects on the environment. The objective of the demand management is to secure the total level of traffic, and its distribution by modes, locations, and times of day that would exist if traffic by each travel mode were to be charged prices equal to its full marginal social cost. With that objective in view all demand management measures aim at increasing the cost of travel, either explicitly through charges like parking fee, congestion charges and fuel prices, or implicitly by limiting traffic through traffic control measures.

Traffic demand can be restrained by using a range of physical measures such as:

- Limiting entry to environmentally sensitive areas;
- Road space reallocation to high occupancy vehicles;
- Traffic calming measures.

While the use of such measures is likely to reduce traffic to some areas, in order to be more effective these should be coupled with measures that encourage use of public transport and pricing. Many developed countries have now levied congestion charges for entry at a particular time into a particular area or are moving towards charging the vehicle use rather than the ownership.

(d) Infrastructure Provision

It is often argued that as the townships expand, so should the road capacity. It is often seen that 10 to 12 percent of land space devoted to all forms of road rights-of-way in the major cities (World Bank 2002). Primary rights-of-way for roads need to be acquired at the outset of any development. The character and capacity of the infrastructure provision has to be tailored to the nature and density of the planned or anticipated developments. Early planning of and reservation of space is thus a necessacity. Cities with only 10 to 15 percent of their area devoted to the transport infrastructure cannot support unlimited motorization. Besides, once the township is established it becomes rather difficult to super impose additional transport infrastructure. Moreover, where congestion is suppressing demand, additional roads normally mean additional traffic and hence more congestion. Thus a strategy that combines necessary road capacity adjustment to support city expansion with clear policies on the allocation and use of the road space is likely to reconcile city expansion with livability (World Bank 2002).

Of particular importance in infrastructure provision would be the poverty focus. It could be achieved by a two-pronged strategy that focuses infrastructure development in the areas inhabited by the poor and strengthening the modes of transport used by the poor. In most of the urban settlements, poor often live in slums having no formal paved roads. Even in the rural areas, they generally live far away from the main settlements and hence are deprived of road connectivity. Absence of road connectivity deprives the rural poor of the mechanized modes of transport leaving them to non-mechanized modes. One of the very common ways of contributing to poverty reduction used in the developing countries is adopting labor intensive methods of road construction and maintenance that generate employment in the rural areas.

5.3 Theory of Road Pricing

Economists often prefer pricing approach to a regulatory approach. Economic theory, in its most classical form, considers prices to be a vital factor in shaping the choices of economic agents, as it is prices that govern the markets on which those decisions are made, and prices that determine supply and demand. They even have a role when the goal is sustainable development. Prices select the most efficient producers (those whose manufacturing costs do not exceed the price) and the most eager consumers (those whose ability to pay does exceed the price) and hence become a way of achieving optimal efficiency, a situation in which no individual's satisfaction can be raised without lowering that of another. This is a natural, automatic process when the economy is operating in competition mode. However, when competition is distorted by externalities, as is often the case with goods administered by government (as transport infrastructure is), market prices must necessarily be adjusted by a public authority to reflect the cost to the community. Prices thus become the best means of achieving the optimal efficiency.

Classical economic theory holds, for instance, that pricing is a more efficient way of restricting the use of a good than setting ceilings on the individual use of that good. The goal will be achieved at the least cost to enterprises by controlling prices rather than quantities in the case of goods used in the production process, or by minimizing consumer satisfaction in the case of final goods. One reason for this can be seen in the different functions of prices:

- The price mechanism supports an efficient allocation of scarce goods (static efficiency).
- Congestion pricing is often mentioned as an efficient means to allocate scarce network capacity.
- Prices set dynamic incentives to change behavioural patterns, to develop new technologies, etc. (dynamic efficiency); they can, *inter alia*, reduce the adverse impacts of transport on the environment and human health.
- Pricing generates revenues that can be used for financing purposes.

In order to calculate the price-relevant marginal cost of road services, the following three-term expression is used as a starting point:

$$P^* = MCprod + Q \frac{dAC}{dQ} + MCext$$

P* = optimal price of road services;

Q = traffic volume;

MCprod = road service *producer* marginal cost;

ACuser = road service *user* average cost (= private marginal cost as perceived by an individual motorist);

MCext = transport *system-external* marginal cost.

Traditional road pricing theory, focused on the problem of too many cars for the available road capacity, has in recent years been supplemented by some arguably even more fundamental aspects of the road capacity. Taking the system externalities into account has consequences not only for optimal road capacity utilization, but also on transport technology itself. Optimal road pricing requires that the relationship between a number of different price-relevant cost items and traffic volume can be determined, rather than just the total costs of each item, which traditional highway cost allocation studies are aiming at.

(a) Social Marginal Cost Pricing (SMCP)

The predominant approach is based on neoclassical micro- and welfare economics and gives therefore special emphasis to efficiency aspects. The advocates of this approach suggest the introduction of a pricing strategy in transport (all modes) that is oriented at short-run social marginal costs. Opponents of this "mainstream approach" criticize the strong focus put on (static) efficiency considerations. They especially highlight the cost recovery requirements to be met by revenues from pricing. In the sense of departures from neoclassical welfare theory, the emphasis is put on "sustainable dynamic schemes of pricing and investment under institutional constraints".

The intention to transfer the basic microeconomic pricing principle of short-run marginal cost pricing (i.e. to introduce a pricing scheme where prices are set equal to the additional costs of an additional kilometer traveled or trip made) is not new but rather re-emerged in the mid-nineties in the political and academic discussion. The striking point of this approach is that short-run SMCP leads to an efficient use of the existing capacity of transport infrastructure. The focus of the recent research work in transport pricing has been on ways to overcome the considerable difficulties connected with implementation of SMCP in transport as it needs comprehensive marginal cost information. The "price-relevant costs" can be arranged in three groups: producer costs, user costs and transport system external costs. For each cost category, difficulties can be found in the cost calculation but also in the resulting price signals. For instance, it is difficult to work out the additional wear and tear cost arising out of an additional vehicle entering the road. Likewise, information about the impacts on cultural and heritage values, forest damage, the recreational value of fauna and flora is still insufficient. Data on marginal accident cost and noise cost is also often not available besides it may even be difficult to isolate the influence of additional vehicle entering the road network as against other factors like the condition of the existing vehicles.

(b) Alternative Pricing Approach

The alternative approach dwells on the premise of treatment of cost recovery: cost recovery ratios should not be a residual variable of a pricing scheme. Pricing in transport should rather be designed in such a way that well-defined cost recovery goals are achieved. The transport infrastructure is considered as a "club good" which should be fully paid by those who use it. Taxpayers should only contribute if there is a special interest by the general public in the provision of the specific infrastructure or service (for example connecting the backward areas). If the users have to pay the full costs - minus public contributions in the case of a special public interest - there is no incentive to overemphasize the need for new infrastructure.

In the case of SMCP, such an incentive exists in situations where the extension leads to lower user prices (e.g. because of lower congestion and lower maintenance costs). The low user prices will not cover the total costs of the extension. The burden is transferred to taxpayers or to users of other, congested parts of the network. Pricing schemes oriented at cost recovery can make private sector involvement in the financing of new transport infrastructure easier. Inter- and intramodal competition in transport does not require that a certain pricing principle is defined for the different transport sectors and modes. Fair competition rather requires the same conditions for all transport providers (no discrimination) and harmonized cost recovery ratios for all transport infrastructure. High prices in urban areas caused by congestion pricing under SMCP can have undesirable impacts on land use by accelerating urban sprawl.

However, road pricing is a form of taxation. Generally, taxes create inefficient allocations in the economy because they drive a wedge between the marginal cost of production and the price the consumer has to pay. The seriousness of this problem differs however between the different kinds of taxes. Too little is known about how transport taxes perform in this respect. Road pricing strategies inevitably produce a large revenue for the government. The social value of this effect depends on the following factors:

1. Does road pricing itself produce distortionary effects in the economy outside of the transport sector?
2. How is the revenue used? Is it used to cut back the most distortionary forms of taxation (like the tax on labour) or to provide a public good for which there is a high willingness-to-pay, or is it used for other purposes than to improve the efficiency of the economy?

5.4 Conclusion

Pricing is a set of measures that can be used to encourage transport system users to behave in a sustainable way. To use this instrument in the most effective way, it must be applied at the most appropriate point of leverage of the system. Today, pricing takes the form of tolls, road pricing, and congestion charging, which is in a way unfair to users as they are forced to use their cars by existing structures which are optimized for individual situations and not for the system (people may be forced to use cars since the nearest bus stop is not within a walking distance or there is no reliable public transport).

Unlike standard goods, which are charged directly to the purchasers, transport goods are often paid for indirectly. The best example of this is road charging. Users pay a tax on oil products, tolls for specific infrastructure, as well as parking fees, tax on car licences, the combination of which actually constitutes road charging. But of course these charges do not exactly match the cost of infrastructure and externalities: they do not vary according to the same parameters, and are not adjusted to reflect congestion density or environmental damage. Some countries have introduced environmental taxes on vehicles according to their pollution or noise levels, but there is room for improvement here as they are usually set-price payments which do not reflect changes in pollution levels depending on factors such as the location of the vehicle, the time of day or roadworthiness.

6

PUBLIC TRANSPORT SYSTEMS

6.1 Introduction

Public transport is one of the most important components of the transport sector and often has an important role in transport policy. Usually considered synonymous to transport for the poor, recent studies in the developed countries have proved that it could be equally popular with the rich people (World Bank 1996). Moreover, it is key to controlling the transport externalities (congestions, pollution and accidents) as failure of public transport generates small vehicle para transit with adverse consequences. With the development of economies, cities develop along with the road infrastructure connecting them. Walking can no longer suffice the major trip requirements of the citizens creating a demand for public transport. As per the World Bank estimates (World Bank 1996), buses are the main mechanized mode carrying 6.5 trillion passenger kilometers per year in 3 million vehicles all over the world. The public transport in most of the developing countries is dominated by the public sector companies with certain degree of privatization.

However, despite its importance and the potential, public transport in many developing countries suffers from serious problems of capacity and quality. Introduction of the public transport often takes place through the public sector monopolies. Being funded through the general budgetary means, initially the public sector monopolies have capacity as the main bottleneck owing to the poor financial condition of the companies. Slowly as the market is opened for the private sector operators, instances of massive over provisioning of capacity are reported in many countries causing the problems of urban congestion and environmental degradation. The most striking reason for decline of the public transport systems arises with the governments attempting to use the public transport industry as an instrument of social policy by simultaneously controlling fare levels and structures and guaranteering favorable wages and working conditions to the employees. The out come is the ever increasing deficits of the service providers and as the deficits mount, in the absence of a secure fiscal basis of subsidy, first maintenance, then service reliability and finally operating capacity disappear (World Bank 2002). World Bank (2002) findings suggest that in the process of decline, public subsidy tends to be captured by a limited group not necessarily from the weaker sections of the society. In cases the beneficiaries are from unionized labor and/or the students.

Discussions in this chapter focus on the importance of public transport systems in the transport policy. Issues involved in managing the public transport are highlighted and policy issues in introducing privatization are examined along with the need for promoting Mass Rapid Transit Systems (MRTS).

6.2 Public Transport Services

One of the key concerns of the transport policy is public transport. Owing to the multiplicity of objectives (social, environmental and economic concerns), a variety of interventions is required making it an area offering the most difficult challenge to the policy makers. These interventions aim at regulating the market for road space either by physical measures legal controls or nascent market mechanisms as well as a variety of regulatory and control measures relating to public transport. Such interventions are intended to have an impact on operations (supply) as well as demand and model split. On the supply side the focus is cost efficiency through the introduction of competition. The competition spectrum includes a number of regulatory regimes namely open competition, deregulation through regulated competition and fully monopolized supply mostly through a public sector company.

In the public monopoly form, transport operations are exclusively by an operator enjoying a permit from the regulatory authorities without competition. Neither is there any competition in the matter of allotment nor is there any competition in operation of the service. The limited competition model offers a variety of private sector participation options. These are in the form of franchise and concessions. Franchise often takes a number of forms like total franchise, operational franchise, management franchise and planning franchises. The deregulated open competition model is the Indian type public service provision. Under the deregulated type no restriction are applied in grant of route permits. The restrictions that the operators face are as per general law on business practices, vehicle construction and use and highway and traffic related restrictions. Licensing is often employed as a surrogate restriction on market access and delivery. These licensing norms regulate quality as well as quantity. The quantity licensing is resorted to by specifying the vehicles allowed to operate in a particular route or area. In the case of quality licensing, the operation of a public transport service is allowed by anyone receiving a permit and complying with conditions attached to the permit.

Economic theory suggests that private firms are likely to be more effective in maximizing profits due to a variety of financial, market and intervention incentives provided by takeover constraints, bankruptcy constraints, shareholder monitoring and lack of outside interference. In terms of labour productivity, the studies in Europe (World Bank 2002) reveal that best performance was achieved by the limited competition systems, where vehicle-kms per member of staff are 8 per cent higher than in deregulated markets and 18 per cent higher than in regulated markets, although this may reflect variations in input prices including labour costs. Competitively tendered franchise however, address two different purposes: control aim and the efficiency aim. The control aim is reflected in a planned system under which transport authorities define route structures, fares and the overall structure of the public transport system. The control role reflects social welfare objectives. The efficiency role seeks to create a more efficient public transport system both in terms of internal efficiency and allocative efficiency.

These two roles can be conflicting. Systems which maximize net social benefits frequently do not give the most internally efficient public transport system. Case study evidence suggests (World Bank 2002) that profit maximization can reduce net economic benefits. In contrast, in certain instances open access (competition-in-the-market) may increase net social benefit, where it leads to new services or new pricing structures. In contrast, competition tends to reduce net social benefits where it leads to supplication of services or excessive price wars. However, public intervention of some sort is likely to be required to maximize welfare due to user economies of scale (user benefit from increased service levels) and second-best arguments (subsidy required to offset the impact of congestion, accidents and environmental pollution by cars).

Issues may also arise over the form of contract and selection of preferred bidder. Competitive tendering may be the most appropriate selection method for operational level decisions but may be less appropriate for tactical and strategic level decisions. Net subsidy contracts should be more efficient than full-cost contracts but this assumes perfect knowledge and/or risk neutrality. Some of these problems and other issues related to mobile and fixed assets can generate barriers to competition. It has been strongly argued that tenders covering both operations and provision and upkeep to assets favor the incumbents particularly at the time of renewal of franchises.

Among the key areas in which governments need to formulate policies prior to privatization are ***price regulations, quality standards, and access regulations***. With reference to price regulations concerns are two fold. First, the pricing regime is required to be dynamic enough to allow for the changes in costs to be compensated for ensuring the recovery of a reasonable return for the private investor. It is especially important in the situation when the private entrepreneur has to co-exist with the public sector and the public sector company is supported by the budgetary support and the market is regulated by a price cap or some kind of incentive based regulatory regime. It has been seen that due to the developing countries being more sensitive to changes in risk levels (owing to reasons of political and economic instability and inconsistency), the investors would naturally expect tariffs to reflect these changes. The second pricing issue relates to the tariff structure. One of the outcomes of interaction between restructuring and fiscal concerns with incidence on prices is cross subsidies. The hidden nature of cross subsidies leaves enough to be desired in terms of their implications and financial impact rendering the private enterprise exposed to the risk if inadequacy of returns or leaving an extraordinary rent.

Introduction of privatization in the transport sector should be well planned and regulated. In designing and developing privatization models, it is essential to prescribe quality standards of performance alongside the price and quantity targets. The quality parameters are often divided into service and no service dimensions. The service aspects of quality include the journey time, service frequency and reliability. The non-service parameters on the other hand include safety and environmental performance. Motivated by the dictum of profit maximization, the private entrepreneurs may compromise on the standards of performance to save on costs. In terms of safety considerations, provision of third party liability insurance, the amount of cover that should be considered necessary and liability and cost recovery allocation in cases of accidents should be clear. Appropriate loading of liability on the operators in case of damage will help keeping them on tenterhooks. Environmental standards are generally set by the national bodies while these are enforced by the regional and local governments. Inappropriate maintenance of fleet often results in greater emissions than the prescribed norms. The permits should incorporate appropriate conditions to ensure a management plan for adherence and permit cancellation to be resorted to in case of repeat violations.

Access regulation is another important area from the point of view of offering a level playing field as some facilities are necessary inputs in the production and process of transport services. For example bus stands, booking and parking places. Unless access pricing rules are defined before the business is passed on to the private operators, the rents may be created that are harmful for the users. Access tariffs are required to be designed to avoid undue discrimination: mostly the dominating public sector undertaking has an upper edge. One very effective solution could be to separate the ownership of access facility and operation of services.

6.3 Public Sector Transport Provisioning

Despite the advantages that the competition offers (cutting cost, providing alternatives and incentives for optimization and improvement in quality), there are certain distinct disadvantages associated with competition in the markets. These mostly emanate from the very basis of the private sector operation. Since it is profit driven, excessive competition is often associated with cutthroat competition resulting in situations such as hanging back to maximize the patronage either on the road or on the terminals, blocking to obstruct rival operator services, racing to beat rival vehicles on picking up passengers, and turning back half way to pick up passengers.

From the perspective of a public sector transport provider, the increased competition brings problems of falling occupancy, price wars and deteriorating service quality affecting emissions and road safety. In addition, certain factors leave a scope for the public sector operation in the market essentially arising out of three factors. First, if there is not sufficient demand for the service, the private sector will not come forward regardless of the desirability of providing connectivity to places. Second, the process of competitions results in provision of a variety of services with different price tags requiring the consumers to a lot of effort in gathering information for making selection. However, given the proportion of expenditure made by an average household on transport in a typical developing country scene (being a very small fraction of the incomes), it may not be desirable by the consumer. Finally, there are often problems in modal integration with the individual private service providers to entertain customers booked by a rival service.

An alternate explanation that put up a strong case in favor of the public sector transport services is treating transport as a merit good. It is argued (Narayan 2000) that the lack of road, transportation and water infrastructure is seen as defining characteristics of poverty. Hence transport policies that improve the general economic viability of the area are considered to be pro poor. This approach aims at transport supply with extensive fare reduction or subsidies to the disadvantaged people. However, the real problem lies in funding the concessions. In case the funding of subsidies is done through budgetary mechanism, financing the deficit budgets may pose even more intricate problem. A possible solution to this problem is cross subsidization of the costs of concessions. There are two specific effects generated by such an approach. First, it implies that some passengers pay more for the same service to fund the trips by the other group. Second, it often ends up generating a large category of passengers who are extended this benefit many of whom may not really deserve.

Considering the Indian scenario, the problem of public transport is often attributed to four factors. First is the problem of confused priorities: conflicting social and economic objectives. The public transport providers are expected to provide service at uneconomic rates and yet generate profits for sustenance. Most of the transport undertakings in the country are organized as corporate entities expected to operate commercially yet obliged to follow the fare structure and the concessions determined by the government mostly on social/political considerations. Second, owing to their inability to operate commercially, the capacity of these road transport corporations to generate resources both internally and externally is substantially curtailed. Low and uneconomic fares coupled with a long category of concessional travelers prohibits cost recovery. Such decision making guided by noncommercial considerations also reduces their capacity to approach institutional lenders for credit. Third, the non-professional working coupled with excessive focus on new investment without much attention to the asset management and optimization renders capacity utilization very weak. Finally, the absence of user's participation in management of the services precludes accountability.

These problems essentially emanate from the strongly held belief that considers transport as a social sector pushing economic efficiency to the back seat. The real irony is that the economic considerations are often compromised in the interest of equity and concern for the poor. Such a strategy often ends up damaging the public transport systems that the poor require the most. The equity guided policies promote public sector monopolies by restricting the entry of the private service providers which in turn result in inefficient use of resources. Low fares, cross subsidies and service controls do not always help the poor. To the contrary, a well managed competition can be pro-poor (World Bank 2002). Competitive service providers guided by purely commercial considerations can be organized with the local governments with an arrangement of direct subsidies. However, the competition has to be introduced in a planned manner. Poorly managed deregulation could be counterproductive: could potentially end up causing congestion, pollution and safety problems.

6.4 Mass Rapid Transport Systems

One of the key justifications for the Mass Rapid Transport Systems (MRTS) is to overcome the typical problems associated with road transport: congestion and pollution. As the economic prosperity in the area rises, the per capita incomes rise and so does the need to travel for business and pleasure. The per capita car ownership in the area increases manifold alongwith the number of trips per person. The existing infrastructure of roads and public transport system starts falling short of the requirement leading to increase in the average travel time and cost of travel.

Besides, the speed of connectivity also assumes importance to retain competitiveness in terms of time factor. Mass Rapid Transport system usually has superior capacity and performance compared with the un-segregated road public transport. It has the potential of contributing to the achievement of all the main development objectives in an urban area. It is capable of improving efficiency of the city economy by reducing travel costs and by maintaining higher level of city centre activity and the associated economies of agglomeration than would be the case in the absence of these (World Bank 2002). It can benefit the poor by providing them the mobility as well as by way of increased economic activity in the area. The quality of life is improved due to shifting of movements to more environmentally begin regions as well as improvement in the quality of environment in the area.

However, how far are the benefits actually derived is a matter of great details. Because there are a wide range of MRT technologies, and pricing and financing mechanism, it depends on the selection of the appropriate one. Often the problem is not simply of selecting the appropriate technology but a matter of selecting the optimum mix and the matter of phasing the development. It has to be ensured that the choices made are consistent with city characteristics, objectives and the economic capabilities. Among the option available in this regard include Bus Rapid Transport (BRT), Light Rails systems, and Metros. The ultimate choice of the system depends on a number of factors. Several MRT technologies are required to be considered to assess there benefits and costs and suitability for a particular area.

6.5 Conclusion

Public regulation of transport services and infrastructure is highly complex task, and basically still in its infancy. Command and control practices predominate even though more effective alternatives exist. Direct intervention regulation and market based interventions should be considered in a subsidiary perspective. Public competition and regulation are not as far apart as is commonly considered. Transport sector is quite peculiar as it abounds with market failures and touches on very sensitive issues and social objectives. The stronger the drive for liberalization, the more public intervention has to be attentive and updated. In other words the more market we want the better the state we need.

7

TRANSPORT SUSTAINABILITY AND POLICY

7.1 Introduction

Comprehensive transport provision is an important input into the efficient functioning of industry, agriculture, and trade. It also affords individuals and households the benefits of mobility and access. A strong policy backing enables the transport systems to be efficient and ensures provisioning of the service to everyone. A policy lays down the basic rules and requirements which can guide all decisions and actions that need to be taken (World Bank 1996) by providing a framework within which decisions can be taken. However, policy has to be determined in conjunction with an overall vision for transport. While this vision could be implicit or explicit, it provides a framework that enables the following different things to be considered together and conceptualized:

- The traveler and mode of travel;
- The infrastructure on which travel takes place;
- The social, economic and environmental context in which the travel takes place.

The traveler and mode of transport relates to the demand side of transport. It is often considered from the perspective of a household. The household demand for travel is divided into two categories: local and long distance travel. While the local travel arises due to the domestic needs emanating from the need to collect water, fuel wood and going to school; the long distance travel often arises due to the need to travel for paid employment, visit to local markets, hospitals and leisure. The household's ability to access the travel mode depends on the availability and affordability factors which account for variation in demand for travel between the developed and developing countries. Other factors influencing the access and mobility are:

- Spatial structure of settlements;
- Cultural variations in demand for goods and services;
- Natural resource endowments;
- Demographic characteristics;
- Type and quality of transport infrastructure;
- Availability of affordable means of transport; and
- Government policy

Transport infrastructure in the less developed countries consists of two complimentary parts: modern and traditional. The modern transport system is a skeletal network of roads, navigable waterways, railways and airways, which is used in main, by the mechanical means of transport. The traditional network has been overlain partly by the modern network. It consists of dense pattern of paths and tracks used by pedestrians and non-motorized modes of transport. It is quite extensive and in most cases the goods and passenger travel undertaken by this mode is equal to the mechanical mode of transport.

The social, economic and environmental context of transport basically arises from the need of sustainability. The *Social* sustainability is concerned with reducing poverty. Poor households derive their standard of living from a variety of activities not all of which are marketed. The transport patterns of poor people exhibit a complex tradeoff among residential location, travel distance, and travel mode in an attempt to minimize the social exclusion associated with low earning capacity (World Bank 2002). In an interesting analysis World Bank report on the City transportation (World Bank 2002) highlights the transport and poverty interrelationship. It is argued that income poor make fewer trips, and more of their trips are undertaken on foot. They have to restrict their requirements to the local markets which makes them *accessibility poor*. As journeys on foot are often more time consuming, it makes them *time poor*. As a pedestrian they are more vulnerable to accidents and violence which makes them *safety poor*. Worst of all is the fact that long distance travel consumes energy making them *energy poor*.

The *economic* sustainability requires that the transport investment should be subject to rigorous cost benefit analysis that encompasses social aspects and environmental externalities. The need for economic justification applies both to infrastructure and to decisions on the purchase and use of vehicles, and the organization of the logistic chain both in public and private sectors. Ensuring the long term sustainability of facilities requires that capital assets are maintained properly. The costs of maintaining excessively ambitious road network and the subsidized operation of poorly managed public transport enterprises in transport also frequently impose unsustainable financial burdens.

The need for *environmental sustainability,* on the other hand, arises as dependence on road transport tends to raise energy consumption, generate air pollution, and have other adverse environmental effects. These adverse environmental effects are difficult to reverse once personal lifestyles and location of activities have been arranged to accommodate a high dependence on personal modes of road transport. The challenge is to devise a transport policy that ensures the actual outcomes are chosen and planned for rather than being the unintended and unforeseen consequences of the policies adopted.

Discussions in the chapter enlist concerns of the transport policy and ways to address them. The issues in sustainability of transport operations are highlighted and towards the end the guiding principles of sustainable transport are discussed.

7.2 Concerns for A Trasport Policy

Among the prime concerns that a transport policy ought to address are:

- Providing infrastructural support in the form of rapid transportation network for transportation of humans and goods;

- Mitigating the external impacts of transportation;
- Providing alternate modes of transportation for alternate places to optimize the benefits and minimize costs;
- Promoting equity and welfare through concessional facilities to the weaker sections and remote areas;
- Promoting road safety; and
- Promoting community participation in transportation sector.

Providing infrastructural support is a gigantic task involving provision of passenger as well as goods transportation facilities to all places in a country/region. Development of other sectors is dependent on the availability of the transport infrastructure. Obviously, this involves a huge investment and it is not always possible to cater to the same from the public resources. It is therefore essential to enlist private participation in providing infrastructural support services. The transport policy has thus to provide an incentive mechanism and the direction to guide the private resources to the desired areas. The policy instruments have also to offer a framework whereby the policies of transport development do not come in conflict with other sectors of the economy. Very often the transport sector is an area of privatization and commercialization policies promoting private sector participation and 'user-pays' principle (World Bank 1996). Owing to this, public sector companies working in the transport sector are privatized and subsidies abolished. Such a policy may come in conflict with that of rural development and poverty alleviation unless suitable safe guards are built in the framework.

Transportation facilities and activities have significant sustainability impacts, including those listed below.

Table 7.1 : Transportation Impacts on Sustainability

Economic	*Social*	*Environmental*
Traffic Congestion; Mobility Barries; Accident Damages; Facility Costs; Consumer Costs; Depletion of Non-Renewable Resources	Inequity Of Impacts; Mobility; Disadvantaged; Human Health Impacts; Community Interaction; Community Livability; Aesthetics.	Air and Water Pollution; Habitat Loss; Hydrological Impacts; Depletion of Non-Resources

Sustainability requires more efficient, equitable, and environmentally sensitive transport including rethinking as to how we measure transportation. While often transport planners treat vehicle movement as an end in itself, the sustainable transportation planning focuses on access, which can often be improved with strategies that reduce the need to travel altogether (such as land use management and improved communications). Sustainability requires comprehensive decision-making that takes into account indirect and interrelated impacts. Sustainable transport planning begins with a community's strategic plan, which individual transportation decisions must support. It requires policies that reward individuals, agencies and communities for achieving sustainability objectives. There are many specific transportation strategies that can help support sustainability, including improved travel choices, more efficient pricing, and more efficient land use. Individually such strategies may have modest impacts, but implemented together they can provide substantial benefits. It is argued (Litman 2003) that a third or more of current motor vehicle use could be reduced by eliminating market distortions that encourage inefficient travel. The transport policy has therefore to aim at this.

Development of alternate modes of transport to provide an efficient service for passenger and freight transport is also among the prime concerns of the transport policy. The emphasis is on development of environment friendly modes and non-motorized modes of transport. To improve the choice, comfort, convenience, frequency and safety of the road passenger transport, it is often suggested (Reddy 2000) that the vehicle design and technology has to be changed. Urban buses should have air suspension, low floor and high carrying capacity and better seats for comfort, and should be fitted with power steering to reduce the fatigue of the driver and thus reduce accidents. More fuel-efficient and environment friendly alternatives like CNG need to be developed at all places to reduce emissions. Another most neglected aspect is that of promotion of non-motorized transport system. In some developed countries efforts are being made to develop and popularize usage of cycling and walk trips by promoting pathways and cycling.

Transport sector could also contribute to poverty relief and promoting equity by improving the ability to access goods, services and employment opportunities. Equity is measured in terms of horizontal equity and vertical equity (Litman 2003). The horizontal equity implies that externalities of transportation should be reduced except where they are specifically justified. This includes reducing pollution emissions and accident risks from motor vehicle use, or compensating those who bear the external costs. It also implies that the users pay for what they get which in turn implies more accurate road and parking fees and insurance pricing. Vertical equity, on the other hand, implies that access options should improve for people who are economically, socially and physically disadvantaged. It often means discounted prices for the disadvantaged. The transport policy has therefore to address both horizontal and vertical equity concerns of the area for which it is framed.

Consultation with potential beneficiaries of intervention is critical from the outset of policy design. As with any appraisal technique, consultation should be a continuing activity over the lifetime of a project or programme, from conception to implementation and monitoring. First and foremost, key stakeholders should be included in a dialogue with local authority and donor representatives before a project of intervention is planned, to ensure that the design of the project involves the most appropriate sectors. Whilst planning for development should be holistic and multi-sectoral, in reality the budgets from which interventions are funded tend to be sectoral. Therefore, whilst the requirements of a community may overlap different sectors, the funding of implementation comes from very distinct sources.

For this reason, it is important to identify as accurately as possible the priority sectors for intervention. This is especially true for the transport sector that cuts across a much wider geographical catchment, as well as being one of the most capital-intensive areas of intervention.

DFID (2003) provides an exhaustive review on the stakeholders in the transport sector. It argues that as transport impacts on every facet of life, the stakeholders of transport are, therefore, the whole community. Furthermore, because of the role of the sector in national development, there are many others outside the context who also have an interest in the development of transport. Categorization of transport stakeholders would include the following:

- Direct transport users (travelling public, shippers, distributive industry)
- Indirect transport users (households, consumers, agricultural producers, health-care providers, education providers)
- Transport facilitators (regulators, roads administrators)
- Transport providers (freight and public transport operators, road construction companies)
- Urban community (consumers, users of facilities)
- National community (defence and geo-political interests)
- External community (importers of produce, multi-national manufacturers and trading companies, tourists).

7.3 Guiding Principles for Sustainable Transportation

Mobility of people, places, goods and services is important to the social and economic well being of communities. Among the key areas of concern from the point of view of sustainability in transportation are:

(a) Access

People are entitled to reasonable access to other people, places, goods and services. Two cardinal principles are followed in improving the access. First principle of transport sustainability relies on reducing the need for travel by changing urban form, promoting new communications technologies, and developing more efficient packaging. It thus ends up reducing the quantity of travel. The second principle is related to the qualitative aspect. The access is sought to be improved by diversifying transportation options, giving people more choices as to how they meet their access needs.

Transportation systems are a critical element of a strong economy, but can also contribute directly to building community and enhancing quality of life.

(b) Equity

The Governments have to strive to ensure social, interregional and inter-generational equity. It requires meeting the basic transportation-related needs of mall people including women, the poor, the rural, and the disabled. Transport is most equitable if it provides the greatest benefit at the least cost to disadvantaged groups, therefore, compensating for overall social inequity. This definition is usually used to oppose price increases and support subsidies. On the other hand, vertical equity with regard to mobility need and ability is a measure of how well an individual's transportation needs are being met compared with others in his community. It assumes that everybody should enjoy at least basic level of access. Horizontal equity is concerned with the fairness of cost and benefit allocation between individuals and groups. Horizontal equity implies cross subsidies and is often cited when the communities compete for transportation resources. It becomes an issue in the allocation of transport funds between geographic jurisdictions because transportation projects provide short term economic stimulations (jobs and contracts) and long term economic development.

(c) Health and Safety

Transportation systems should be designed and operated in a way that protects the health (physical, mental and social well-being) and security of all people, and enhances the quality of life in communities. Health and safety aspects of transportation in the form of environmental impacts, accidental impacts and psychological impacts arising out of accidents and driving stresses due to congestion. As all these essentially relate to externalities of transport, these are sought to be minimized by the transport policy with the help of instruments discussed in chapter 4.

Security is another aspect that has gained significance in the recent past. Threats to security of person and property are classified into four groups. First is theft by stealth. It is largely a function of overcrowding in public service vehicles. Second, is theft by force. It may occur in crowded places or in the situations when the victim is isolated. Third, is sexual harassment which can occur in both crowded and isolated places. Finally is act of violence in which transport is coincidental.

(d) Holistic Transport Planning

Transportation decision makers have a responsibility to pursue more integrated approaches to planning. Some useful tips for this would include:

- Concentrating urban growth, limiting sprawl and providing for more mixed land use through urban structure and land use policies. This would reduce demand (especially for automobile trips) by moving origins and destinations closer together and also help reduce habitat destruction and loss of agricultural and recreational lands.
- Giving priority to less polluting, lower impact modes of transportation in the design of transportation systems and urban areas. Pedestrian and cycling paths should be provided as attractive and safe alternatives to cars.
- Maintaining and enhancing the health and viability of urban public transit systems.
- Integrating transport modes, whether for passengers or goods, in order to provide more efficient goods movement, and to increase the availability of lower impact transportation options such as public transit.

- Protecting historical sites and archaeological resources, reduce noise pollution, and consider aesthetics in the planning, design and construction of transportation systems.
- Ensuring public and private sector stakeholders coordinate their transportation planning, development and delivery activities. These transportation decisions should also be integrated with environment, health, energy and urban land-use decisions.
- Making transportation-related decisions in an open and inclusive process by informing the public about transportation options and impacts, and encourage them to participate in decision making so that the needs of different communities (i.e. rural vs. urban; cyclists vs. drivers, etc.) can be understood and accounted for.
- Adopting a proactive approach rather than the reactionary approach to environmental or social impacts of transportation-related decisions. This will result in considerable cost savings since transportation decisions often involve costly, long-term infrastructure investments.

As human activities can overload the environment's finite capacity to absorb waste, physically modify or destroy habitats, and use resources more rapidly than they can be regenerated or replaced, it is argued that efforts should be made to develop transportation systems that minimize physical and biological stress, staying within the assimilative and regenerative capacities of ecosystems, and respecting the habitat requirements of other species.

(e) Land and Resource Use

Transportation systems must make efficient use of land and other natural resources while ensuring the preservation of vital habitats and other requirements for maintaining biodiversity. It will require:

- Minimizing transportation-related air emissions and discharges of contaminants to surface (fresh and salt water) and ground water.
- Minimizing the generation of waste through each phase of the life-cycle of transportation vehicles, vessels and infrastructure. (reduce, reuse and recycle).
- Ensuring that the rate of use of renewable resources does not exceed rates of regeneration, and non-renewable resource use is minimized.
- Reducing fossil fuel consumption and emissions through efficiencies and demand management.
- Promoting the use of alternative and renewable energy.

Sustainable transportation systems must be cost effective. If adjustment costs are incurred in the transition to more sustainable transportation systems they should be equitably shared, just as current costs should be more equitably shared.

(f) Fuller Cost Accounting

Transportation decision makers must move as expeditiously as possible toward fuller cost accounting, reflecting the true social, economic and environmental costs, in order to ensure users pay an equitable share of costs. This will require:

- Identifying and recognizing public subsidies to all modes of transport and make transportation decisions accordingly.
- Reflecting the full social, economic and environmental costs (including long term costs) of each mode of transport or transport related practice as accurately as possible in market prices.
- Ensuring users pay a fuller share of all costs, while respecting equity concerns.
- Promoting research and development of innovative alternative technologies that improve access and help protect the environment. The emphasis should be on providing a wide range of transportation options.
- Considering the potential economic and employment benefits that could be derived from the restructuring of our transportation systems.

7.4 Conclusion

A great deal of mobility now a days is forced mobility often arising out of our inability to incorporate transport planning in the planning of urban forms and infrastructure. In the passenger traffic segment educational, professional or business travel, and leisure travel accounts for the growing travel demand. The freight transport however, is rising as a result of growing distribution of labour with intensive outsourcing processes are responsible for the growing freight transport demand. Globalization is leading to exploitation of cost saving potential and improvement in customer oriented quality of delivery is putting pressure on the transport sector. It is important therefore that the transport processes and the individual modes endeavour to cope with such complexity. The expectations from the transport policy thus increase tremendously.

Besides, sustainability is both a duty and an obligation for the transport sector. This is underlined by the accumulation of external effects with the requirements for mobility growing day by day. The derived nature of transport demand makes it very difficult for the planners to control the transport demand with the help of tools of transport economics and policy. It could only aim at mitigating the external effects of transport and to a certain extent curb the need to travel by resorting to an effective transport planning.

8
ROAD TRANSPORT IN HIMACHAL PRADESH: POLICY OPTIONS FOR SUSTAINABLE DEVELOPMENT

8.1 Introduction

In this chapter two prime concerns in the transport and communication sector are addressed: the road infrastructure and policy and the transport sector growth and issues. The theoretical framework of transport economics is reviewed to analyze the problems and find out appropriate policy solutions. While focus of the discussions is Himachal Pradesh, examples from other states (of the Indian Union) and other countries are drawn to highlight the issues.

The chapter is organized as follows. Discussed in the chapter present road network in the state, its growth trends and the concerns and options; overview of the transport sector in the state, the key areas of concern and the policy options. Finally, the conclusions of the study. It is concluded that the ultimate goal of a transport policy should be to use road space efficiently, and allow users to take into account the true cost of their decisions to maximize social welfare. Given the wide variety of measures and technical possibilities, combined with growing seriousness of excessive fuel consumption, congestion and environmental impacts; this challenge could be overcome. It will however, require institutional reforms adopting integrated planning methods and coordinate implementation, development of suitably skilled manpower and, access to substantial financial resources.

8.2 Development of Road Infrastructure

Most transport (be it public or private, passenger or freight, and motorized or non motorized) uses the road system. The road transport is growing at an unusual rate of 10-12 percent per annum. A recent survey showed (Kanchan et.al. 2006) that road transport sector turn over (freight charges) is Rs. 70000 crore per annum with 10,00,000 trucks traveling every day on roads. Serving a land area of 3.3 million square km and a population of one billion, India's transport system is one of the largest systems in the world. Road transport accounts for 80 per cent share of land transport demand.

However, despite its importance, the road system is usually managed in a fragmented and uneconomic way. Decisions on the management, expansion and maintenance of the roads networks are generally taken by a gamut of agencies ranging from the state Public Works Departments, to local urban bodies, Block Development agencies and the Panchayats. It is estimated (MORTH 2005) that of the total roads in India (24.66 Lakh Kms), 42.6 percent are Panchayat roads, 38 percent are PWD roads, 9.4 percent are urban roads and 10 percent are project roads. Akin to the supply side, on the demand side are the small individual entities mostly in the private sector. The worst problem arises with its being a public good. Its feature of being a public good does not allow the normal market mechanism to function with the price regulating the demand and supply in the market. Such a situation of market failure results in juxtaposition of extremely buoyant private demand demonstrated by high levels of congestion and cash starved infrastructure supply agency.

Table 8.1: Road Network (National Highways) in India

Periods	*Total Length (Kms)*	*Widening to two lanes (Kms)*	*Widening to four lanes (Kms)*
1949-69	24000	14000	Nil
1969-90	33612	16000	267
1990-97	34298	3138	483
1997-2002	58112	1955	710
2002-03	58112	710	418
2003-04	65569	671	799
2004-05	65569	221	841

Source: MORTH (2005).

The scene in Himachal Pradesh is no different: there are four agencies handling roads. The National Highways are looked after by the Government of India, the State Highways by the state PWD, town roads by the Municipal bodies and rural roads partly by the PWD and partly by the Rural Development Department. There is unfortunately no agency to coordinate between these which often work in a compartmentalized manner. The development of roads in the state since the formation of state has been as under:

Table 8.2: Road Infrastructure in Himachal Pradesh

Plan period	*Road length (in Kms)*
1951-56	504
1956-61	1300
1961-66	2114
1966-69	6196
1969-74	9042
1974-79	10394
1980-85	13637
1985-90	15560
1992-97	18376
1997-2002	20837
2002-03	23436

Source: Planning Department (2003):194-95.

On an average about 2500 kilometers of road length is added every five years in the state. The growth rate of road network was higher in the initial years of development, which slowed down in the subsequent years as after the basic connectivity at the district and subdivision level was provided, the demand for funds for other sectors of the economy like health, education and social services increased.

Table: 8.3: Category of Roads in Himachal Pradesh

Sr.No.	*Category of Road*	*Single Lane*	*Double Lane*	*Total*
1.	National Highways	486	749	1235
2.	Border Roads	422	269	691
3.	State highways	901	617	1518
4.	Rural Roads	19291	701	19992
	Total	**21100**	**2336**	**23436**

Source: Planning Department (2003): 194-95.

Over 90 percent of the road network consists of single lane roads. With the high growth rate of vehicle population and use, the problems of congestion arise.

Among the key concerns in construction of roads are inadequacy of funds, lack of technical capacity for construction, and high cost of construction. Condition on the maintenance front is even more serious. It is estimated (MORTH 2005) that out of the total road length of 65569 km in India, about 25000 km is under severe strain due to heavy traffic. The allocation of budget on account of maintenance of roads in the central sector is only 40 percent of the requirement. The position in the state sector is expected to be still worse. Owing to a persistent demand for connectivity, often a major share of the budget allocated to the Public Works Department is spent on developing new roads. Being a hilly terrain, per kilometer expenditure on roads in the state is far higher than the plains. There is, therefore, a tendency to under fund maintenance. Among the main issues in the maintenance of roads in the context of Himachal Pradesh are: preparation of road inventories, analysis of defects, determination of requirements and type of interventions, arranging financial resources and preparation of maintenance plans. Any sound road policy ought to address these issues.

The Government of India has attempted to generate resources for maintenance of roads through taxation. The following initiatives have been specifically taken for this purpose.

(a) Increasing the General Fuel Cess

Such a surcharge is often levied on automotive fuels. At present a fuel cess of Rs. 3 per liter is being levied. It is suggested (World Bank 1996) that financing the funding gap through fuel cess would require the cess to be at the level of Rs. 7.5 per litre. Even the state government is charging Rs. 1 per litre cess on fuel.

There is often a strong economic case in favor of levying a higher cess on the diesel as the variable costs imposed by the heavy commercial vehicles is 7-10 times higher than the passenger cars. Heavy trucks are undercharged as against the damage they inflict on roads. One major drawback of such a levy is that it will increase the price differential between diesel and kerosene and encourage fuel adulteration. Another complication is in terms of its impact on the non-road users. It is estimated that 46 per cent of diesel is consumed in non-road application like railways, power plants and irrigation purposes.

However, the funds so received are currently being credited to the general revenues and no separate fund has been created. It is therefore suggested that the state government could establish a dedicated fund to finance the maintenance of state highways and district/ rural roads.

(b) Tolling the National/ State Highways

Road tolls generate a small fraction of the total revenue from road users (about 1%). However, nationally there is a growing interest in directly pricing for road use both to raise revenue and to relate user charges more directly to user costs. There are two constraints in implementing the tolling of roads. First, relates to the cost of collection. There is a certain level of administrative and physical infrastructure required for collection of toll on roads. It is estimated that traffic flows of about 5000 PCUs per day are sufficient to make tolling financially viable. Second, tolls deter marginal users and encourage use of non-toll routes.

On the public acceptability of tolls, a revealed preference survey on Mumbai-Pune expressway and the parallel untolled road revealed that the toll route is preferred by cars, taxis, buses and vans due to time savings. A 25 per cent increase in the toll would divert one third of traffic, while 25 percent reduction could divert about a third more traffic from the untolled road. In the light of present low willingness to pay it may be appropriate to keep the rate so toll ow however, apply them on all vehicles.

The traffic management measures that may be useful in the context of Himachal Pradesh are roadside parking management, traffic circulation measures, bus service priority and regulatory measures under the Motor Vehicles Act. To prevent roadside parking of vehicles, it is essential that special parking areas are developed. The basic cause of lack of parking facilities in India is that it is presumed that parking has to be provided at a social cost without any additional charge to the users. However, the biggest limitation with this assumption is that often funds are not available from the public resources to provide this facility since no bank loan would be available for a venture with no returns. To facilitate parking areas to come up, it may be appropriate to treat parking space as a normal commodity such as gas or electricity, and to follow the implications of a commercial or market approach for prices and investment policy. However, traffic management cannot be seen as a one-shot measure. It needs to be seen as a continuous process. Otherwise, the benefits of congestion reduction achieved by any such intervention will be overtaken by the increasing population of vehicles. Emphasis therefore has to be on creating a favorable institutional environment that encourages effective operation and development of technical skills to implement new techniques.

The economic rationale of demand management is that if the price directly incurred by travelers in making journeys is lower than the full cost of the journey, then some trips will impose a net cost to the community. The full cost of a trip includes personal cost borne by the traveler and the social costs imposed by the traveler on the community in the form of contribution to congestion, the increase in accident potential, and the polluting effects on the environment. The objective of the demand management is to secure the total level of traffic, and its distribution by modes, locations, and times of day that would exist if traffic by each travel mode were to be charged prices equal to its full marginal social cost. With that objective in view all demand management measures aim at increasing the cost of travel, either explicitly through charges like parking fee, congestion charges and fuel prices, or implicitly by limiting traffic through traffic control measures.

Physical restraint measures used in transport management so far have now become ineffective as with the rising population of vehicles and expansion in the road network, it is increasingly becoming difficult to cope with the rising demand of enforcement agencies. Therefore, the trend internationally now is to use charges on vehicle use in place of police powers. Introduction of charges has a double dividend property: they generate financial resources while controlling traffic. Receipts from an entry tax in the Manali town in Himachal Pradesh prove the point.

It is often argued that as the townships expand, so should the road capacity. Early planning of and reservation of space is thus a necessacity. Cities with only 10 to 15 percent of their area devoted to the transport infrastructure cannot support unlimited motorization. Besides, once the township is established it becomes rather difficult to super impose additional transport infrastructure. Moreover, where congestion is suppressing demand, as is the case with most towns in Himachal Pradesh, additional roads normally mean additional traffic and hence more congestion. Thus a strategy that combines necessary road capacity adjustment to support city expansion with clear policies on the allocation and use of the road space is likely to reconcile city expansion with livability (World Bank 2002).

Of particular importance in infrastructure provision would be the poverty focus. It could be achieved by a two-pronged strategy that focuses infrastructure development in the areas inhabited by the poor and strengthening the modes of transport used by the poor. One of the very common way of contributing to poverty reduction used in the developing countries is adopting labour intensive methods of road construction and maintenance that generate employment in the rural areas.

8.3 Transport Sector in Himachal Pradesh

(A) The Policy Regime

All matters relating to registration of motor vehicles, grant of permits, fitness certificates, driving licenses and adherence to the pollution norms are dealt in India under the Motor Vehicles Act 1988 and rules made there under. This work is handled by the Transport Departments and the State and Regional Transport Authorities set up under the Act. These Authorities are responsible for grant of permits and control of motor vehicles in their respective jurisdictions. There has been a drastic change in the way in which matters relating to grant of permits of transport vehicles and their fitness are handled ever since the new Motor Vehicles Act 1988 came into being. The precursor of this Act (the Motor Vehicles Act, 1939) relied on a total command and control regime and assigned a major role to the State Transport Undertakings (STUs) leaving very little room for the private sector. With the amended version of the Motor

Vehicles Act 1988, the entire transport management has undergone a sea change.

The current policy regime can be studied in two parts: legal and institutional framework and fiscal policy related to motor vehicles.

The Motor vehicles operation in the state are governed by the provisions of the Motor Vehicles Act (the Act) and rules made there under. Transport Authorities constituted under the Act decide grant of permits for commercial vehicles of all kinds. The current scenario in respect of the permits of different kinds is given as under:

(a) Stage Carriage Permits

Under this category are vehicles which cater to the day to day commuters carrying them from one place to another. It is called stage carriage as these vehicles often stop at different stages enroute to enable the passengers to board or alight. The Transport Authorities granting permits can not refuge the grant of permit under normal circumstances. The number of buses in the market is determined by the level of competition with weaker firms leaving the market when the competition becomes intense. The fare structure is either market determined or is fixed by the government under the provisions of the Act. The act therefore envisages a situation akin to perfect competition or contestable markets in this sector with free entry and exit from the market and price being pre-determined.

At present there are 1700 buses with the State Road Transport Corporation (HRTC) and 2800 buses in the private sector. Among the key concerns in the Stage Carriage segment are:

(i) While the Himachal Pradesh Road Transport Corporation is constituted to provide connectivity to all places in Himachal Pradesh, its operators are mostly uneconomical with high costs of operations not being re-covered from the fare rates fixed by the government. It has annual losses to the tune of Rs. 70 crore with accumulated losses touching Rs. 400 crores;

(ii) The Corporation is loaded with a long list of concessional passengers some of them traveling free of cost which has badly affected its operations. Despite the annual Grant-in-Aid of Rs. 50 crore and capital investment of Rs. 11.50 crore, it is not even in a position to maintain its fleet and provide service efficiently;

(iii) Apart from the problems of high staff costs, a large number of un-economic routes connecting interior areas with low traffic potential, concessional travelers; it faces intense competition from the private operators and the para transit vehicles. A large number of cabs and maxi-cabs operating in the interior areas poach into its potential travelers resulting in low occupancy and low returns;

(iv) The private sector operation suffers from the drawbacks typical of private sector operations with buses resorting to the following practices:

- Hanging back at stops to maximize passengers (a problem mostly reported from bus stops and other important boarding points);
- Blocking to obstruct the operators services:
- Racing to beat rival's vehicles in picking up passengers; and
- Turning back from busy centres instead of going to the final destinations (especially when these places are in the interior areas).

For tackling these problems the Transport Policy 2004 makes it mandatory for the operators to get a satisfactory operation certificate from the Presidents of Panchayats in rural areas.

(v) Owing to the problems of high taxes on the luxury vehicles, there are very few luxury services operating in the State and most of those in operation connect Delhi with various tourist places in the State. Connectivity is also low during the night hours which results in under utilization of the road infrastructure during the off peak time (8.00 PM – 8 AM); and

(vi) Most of the private sector operation is on the national and state highways with rural and interior areas left to the HRTC.

(b) Goods Carriage Vehicles

The goods carriage permits are also granted by the Transport Authorities on request from the applicants freely. Freight rates are either market determined or are fixed by the government. Sunk costs are not very high hence the operators are free to enter or leave the market as per their business conditions. Number of vehicles operating in the market at any point of time is determined by the market. Again it represents a situation akin to perfect competition or contestable markets.

Goods Carriage operation in the state is characterized by excess supply (vehicles are mostly more than required), cartelization of suppliers in the form of truck unions, competition with small sized vehicles, and problems in freight rates fixation. There are about 50,000 trucks of various sizes operating in the state all of whom are in the private sector. The key issues in this segment are:

(i) A review of the current permit regime is required where grant of permits is very liberal and there are no ceilings on maximum number of trucks for any area. This has resulted in problems of low vehicle utilization leading to high fixed costs per kilometer, cut throat competition among vehicles of various capacities leading to problems of low per vehicle returns and high bank defaulters;

(ii) In the absence of a maximum life prescribed for goods carriage, the market is dominated by aged fleet with low fuel efficiency and high energy consumption;

(iii) There is an acute problem of over loading. It is estimated (Kanchan et al 2006) that an axle carrying double the legal load, may cause from 16 to 60 times as much damage as that of a one legal axle load;

(iv) Over 95 percent vehicles in the state are rigid axle vehicles. The multi-axle vehicles are yet to be introduced; and

(v) These are serious problems in fixation of freight rates and their actual implementation in the market. Incidents are disputes between the truck unions and the industrial houses are on the rise.

(c) Contract Carriage Vehicles

Meant to carry passengers from one point to another on contract basis, the vehicles in this category cater mostly to the passengers in luxury travel segment for leisure and tourism. Also called tourist vehicles, the grant of permits in this category is also liberal, however, in practice the market is dominated by a few big operators. The operators in this segment have to market their product like any other consumer product and can charge prices depending upon their product features and market conditions. Unlike stage carriage or goods carriage vehicles, sunk costs in this segment are higher hence leaving the market is not very easy. Market structures in this category resemble those of monopolistic competition or oligopoly.

Contract Carriage Vehicles are available in various sizes starting from three seater auto-rickshaws to 35-40 seater luxury coaches. Main problems in the sector are:

(i) This segment is faces with increased pressure of new entrants because of the limited avenues of non-form employment available elsewhere. Owing to this, it is probably the segment with highest growth rate (touching 20 to 25 percent). It is causing the problems of intense competition and under utilization of vehicle fleet;

(ii) Owing to the tax advantages available in the segment, there is a common tendency of poaching into the area of Stage Carriage Vehicles; and

(iii) Problems of overcharging and fleecing are commonly reported due to the absence of pre-paid taxi system or metering of taxis.

(d) Private Service Vehicles

Permits in this category are basically meant for firms, educational institutions and corporate houses to cater to their own captive demand.

These vehicles are basically meant to cater to the requirement of private firms or industrial units. As per the provisions of the Act, the vehicles are required to be in the ownership of the firm or institution and can be plied for carrying its staff or students. The main problems in this segment are:

(i) In the absence of a clear cut policy from the Government, private institutions setting up industries or educational institutions have no incentive to own their own buses or trucks. As a result, as more and more educational institutions are coming up in the state, the pressure on the HRTC for providing buses is increasing; and

(ii) There are serious demand and supply mismatches caused due to the sudden growth of industrial areas and sport in new educational institutions in the state.

All transport vehicles are subject to Inspection and Maintenance (IM) checks conducted by the officers of the Transport Department at regular intervals. Currently these tests are carried out visually without much mechanical assistance. Enforcement of the provisions of the Act is done by the Transport Department, Police, and the Courts. While the Act lays down norms for maximum pollution emissions, regrettably, the enforcement is totally ineffective in the face of mass violations. Further, the Act makes little contribution to mitigate traffic congestion and improve road safety.

(B) Motor Vehicles Taxation Policy of Himachal Pradesh

The structure and incidence of taxes and fees that the motor vehicles registered and operating in the state are liable to pay varies with the type of vehicle, cost of vehicle and its area of operation. Among the major taxes are token tax, passenger tax and the special road tax. *Token tax* is akin to a license fee that the owners are supposed to pay in lieu of the usage of road by them. The rates of token tax vary with the kind of use the vehicle is likely to be put to. There are two distinct categories under this kind of a tax: personalized vehicles and the commercial vehicles. The personalized vehicles are under one time taxation regime, that is, they pay tax at the time of registration for a period of 15 years. The commercial vehicles, on the other hand, pay tax on an annual basis. The rates and incidence of tax also vary between these two categories. While the personalized vehicles pay tax in lump sum calculated as certain percentage of the price of the vehicle and collected once in 15 years, the commercial vehicles have to pay tax annually charged on per seat basis in case of passenger vehicles and on a lump sum amount based on the gross weight of the vehicle in case of goods carriers. The rates of the Special Road Tax vary depending upon the nature of the road with users of the national highways paying the highest rates per seat per kilometer and users of the rural roads paying the lowest rates per seat per kilometer.

Like the Special Road tax for the Stage Carriage buses, there is a passenger and goods tax charged from the cabs, tourist buses and the goods carriers. The contract carriages (cabs and buses) pay passenger tax charged on quarterly basis depending upon the seating capacity of the vehicle, the goods carriages are liable to pay goods tax charged on a lump sum basis at varied rates depending upon the class of vehicle (Light Commercial Vehicle, Medium Goods Vehicle and the Heavy Goods Vehicle). In addition, all vehicles pay different fees like the registration fee, special registration fee, permit fee, inspection fee, license fee and the composite fee. All these fees, except the registration fee, are charged on a lump sum basis irrespective of the cost, size and the mechanical strength of the vehicle.

As any analysis of the Motor Vehicles Taxation policy in the state would reveal, the policy does not reflect any clear-cut strategy to achieve any definite objective or to handle transport externalities. The existing tax structure should be simplified first, by minimizing the ambiguities in vehicle classification and the basis of charges. Certain taxes which are difficult to administer like the passenger and goods tax can easily be merged with token tax to make them a single charge. It may be appropriate to say that the state has not used tax as an instrument of control. Instead, it has been used only for generating resources. A few examples of the taxation policy being contrary to the transport policy objectives are seen in the tax structures of personalized vehicles vis-à-vis the public service vehicles, and tax rates in different categories of the public service vehicles. The personalized vehicles are growing rapidly and causing problems of traffic congestion and pollution, however, still the personal vehicles are charged one time tax at nominal rates while the commercial vehicles pay taxes annually. Further, with the rates of token tax of personalized vehicles being a ratio of the price of the vehicle, vehicles conforming to Euro II norms and having state of the art safety features cost more and hence end up paying more taxes whereas cheaper vehicles using obsolete technology creating more pollution and unsafe travel pay less taxes.

Even amongst the commercial vehicles also, the tax disparities raise issues of equity and efficiency. For example, there is a huge gap between the taxes on passenger buses and heavy freight vehicles. The current practice of overcharging the buses and undercharging the freight vehicles has negative implications for both transport efficiency and equity besides imposing extra burden on the roads. The present practice of charging road tax and passenger tax on nominal basis is a blunt instrument as it fails to take account of vehicles with different levels of utilization. In addition, a simple charge based on the Gross Vehicle Weight (GVW) may give distorted signals with reference to the choice of vehicles. New Zealand has addressed this issue by having charges relating to both vehicle weight and distance traveled. Most countries in Europe are also moving in the same direction. Switzerland and Austria have recently implemented network wide weight/ distance charging systems for the trucking industry, with the charge revenue dedicated to road maintenance.

8.4 Areas of Concern

(a) Vehicle Population and Growth Rates

The growth rates of vehicles in the state have been quite phenomenal (from an average growth rate of 2.7 per cent during 1980-85, the annual growth rate of vehicle population increased to 7.8 per cent in 1995-2000). After 1998, the annual growth rates of vehicle population further increased to 12 percent with the availability of easy finance and new models getting launched in the market. The vehicle population, as on end December 2003, comprised of the following:

Table 8.4: : Motor Vehicle Population in Himachal Pradesh

SR.NO.	*CATEGORY OF VEHICLE*	*POPULATION*	*AS PERCENTAGE TOTAL*
1	TWO WHEELERS	149,286	58
2	CARS&JEEPS	63,249	24
3	TRUCKS	37,805	14
4	BUSES	4,417	2
5	THREE WHEELERS	2,611	1
6	OTHERS	3,656	1
	TOTAL	**261,024**	**100**

Source: DOT (2003).

Two wheelers and cars comprised 82 percent of the total vehicle population. The commercialized vehicles were only 25 percent of the total vehicle population. The motor vehicle population in Himachal Pradesh is thus rising with higher shares of personalised vehicles. Within the personalised vehicles as well, the share of two wheelers is very high (about 60 percent). This composition of vehicle population coupled with high growth rates of personalised vehicles has caused serious problems of congestion, accidents and pollution. This raises an important issue: in order to ensure good mobility should we encourage the personal vehicles to grow as they are doing now by providing adequate road space and right of way or should the greater use of public transport be encouraged. Though the data on road space utilization and pollution in the state is not available, going by the national averages, the public transport utilizes much lesser road space and causes less pollution compared to the personalized transport.

Table 8.5: Vehicle Wise Road Space Utilization and Pollution in India

Type of Vehicle	*Average Passengers per Vehicle*	*Pollution Load in gm/passenger per Kilometer*	*Congestion effect in PCU*/ passenger*
2 Stroke 2 Wheeler Petrol Engine	2	7.13	0.375
4 Stroke 2 Wheeler Petrol Engine	2	4.76	0.375
Car with Catalytic Converter Petrol Engine	4	0.93	0.25
Bus with Diesel Engine	40	1.00	0.075

* PCU = Passenger Car Unit where 1 car = 1PCU, 1 Bus = 2.5 PCU, 1 Scooter =0.75 PCU

Source: MORT (2003): 3

Though cars and buses have the same pollution effect on a per passenger basis, buses have the advantage of occupying far less road space. On the other hand, two wheelers not only have a far more damaging effect on the environment than cars and buses, but are also undesirable from a congestion point of view. Hence, from the table above, buses are clearly more desirable and two wheelers are the least desirable. The transport policy has therefore to support investments in facilities that would wean people away from the use of personal vehicles rather than build facilities that would encourage greater use of personal motor vehicles. This would also require a tax and fee regime that discourages the ownership and use of personalized vehicles.

The increased vehicle population is often attributed to two factors. First, with liberalized licensing regime coupled with availability of easy finance, the ability of the middle class to own a vehicle improved substantially. Second, lack of a comfortable, reliable and safe public transport system. Frequent and irregular stops for passenger loading and unloading and lack of dedicated bus lanes contribute to serious traffic congestion and increased fuel consumption. These features increase the journey and waiting time and vehicles are often overcrowded, resulting in increased preference for personalized transport.

(b) Transport Sector and the Socio-economic Priorities

With 30 percent of its population living below the poverty line (E & S 2003), the equity and welfare aspects of transport management also gain significance in Himachal Pradesh. It is often argued

(World Bank 2002) that the transport patterns of the poor people exhibit a complex tradeoff among residential location, travel distance, and travel mode, in an attempt to minimize social exclusion associated with low earning capacity. The World Bank (2002) analyses the role of transport in the concept of exclusion. The income poor make fewer trips, which restricts them to whatever services that are available at walking distance making them 'accessibility poor'. As walking consumes time and energy, it makes them 'time poor' and 'energy poor'. As they are more vulnerable to accidents, they are 'safety poor' as well. Therefore, transport becomes a merit good making its minimum supply a social imperative.

However, as concessions are extended to the poorer sections of the society, the public transport managed by the Public Sector Undertakings (PSUs) suffer heavy losses (MORT 2003). These losses are attributed to the fact that since public transport is mostly used by the poorer sections of the society, it is difficult for the management of these PSUs to increase fares. However, with low fares, it is difficult to recover costs of operation because of which adding capacity becomes an issue. Hence, first maintenance, then service reliability and finally operating capacity disappear. It is therefore imperative to keep a balance between business needs and the equity considerations. Among the alternatives suggested to overcome the problem are introduction of dual pricing system by offering different services to the poor section and the upper income group; private sector participation in the provision of services; and budgetary funding of the deficits of PSUs.

(c) Road Safety

Many developing countries including India have serious road accident problems. Fatality rates are quite high in comparison to the developed world. However, the nature of the problem in the developing countries is much different: the proportion of commercial vehicles involved in accident is much higher and pedestrian and cyclists are often more vulnerable. Although number of deaths per 10000 vehicles is declining in India even then it is much higher in comparison to the developed world. As per a study (Mohan 2004), the number of serious injuries are estimated to be 15 times as many as fatalities whereas simple injuries are about the 70 times the fatal accidents making the ratio as 1: 15: 70. The leading causes of mortality and disability adjusted life years (DALYs) – a health gap measure that combines information on the number of years lost from premature death with the loss of health from disability – in India shows traffic accidents (Table 1) as one of the 10 top causes. By 2020, road deaths and injuries are predicted to be the third leading contributor to the global burden of disease and injury.

Table 8.6: Traffic Fatalities in India in 2002

Deaths			*DALYs*		
Rank	*Cause*	*Percentage of Total*	*Rank*	*Cause*	*Percentage of Total*
1	Ischaemic heart disease	13.9	1	Perinatal conditions	9.2
2	Lower respiratory Infections	9.4	2	Lower respiratory Infections	7.3

3.	Cerebrovascular disease	7.2	3	Ischaemic heart disease	4.9
4	Perinatal conditions	6.9	4	Unipolar depressive Disorders	4.8
5	Tuberculosis	4.7	5	Diarrhoeal diseases	4.8
6	Chronic Obstructive Pulmonary Disease	4.5	6	Tuberculosis	3.7
7	Diarrhoeal diseases	4.1	7	Catracts	2.6
8	HIV/AIDS	2.6	8	HIV/AIDS	2.6
9	**Road Traffic Injuries**	**2.0**	9	Cerebrovascular disease	2.4
10	Diabetes Mellitus	1.8	**10**	**Road Traffic Injuries**	**2.4**

As per the information supplied by the Railway and Traffic wing of Himachal Pradesh road accidents are growing at a rate of 12 to 15 percent per annum, the casualties are growing at the rate of 18 to 20 percent per annum (R&T 2003). There are 11 deaths per 10,000 vehicles in the state (as against 20 in India) which is far higher than 1.2-1.5 per 10,000 vehicles in the developed countries (World Bank 1996). In addition are those suffering serious injuries in road accidents and requiring medical attention. While no estimates of losses due to accidents are available in GDP terms, it is believed that increasingly accidents are causing more damage to the society.

Table 8.7 : Road Accidents and Casualties in Himachal Pradesh

Year	*Total*	*Persons Injured*	*Persons Died*
2000	2055	4302	820
2001	3163	5213	960
2002	2459	4171	616
2003	2702	4291	819
2004	2946	4406	769

Source: Railway and Traffic Wing (2003).

Seen in terms of damage caused due to accidents, the intensity of damage in the state is far higher than the national average. As against the average national accident severity index of 10, the state average is 30.

Table 8.8 : Accident Severity Index

Years	*Accidents*	*Fatalities*	*ASI**
2000	2055	820	40
2001	3163	960	30
2002	2459	616	25
2003	2702	819	30
2004	2946	769	26

* ASI is accident severity index defined as number of fatalities per 100 accidents.

Owing to the concentration of traffic on national highways, over 35 per cent of these accidents occur on the national highways followed by 31 percent on the state highways and 34 percent in other rural roads. Going into the causes of accidents makes an interesting reading.

Table 8.9: Causes of Accidents in Himachal Pradesh

Cause	*Percentage of the total accidents*
Fault of the Driver	36
Mechanical Faults	21
Bad road condition	26
Fault of the pedestrian	11
Natural calamity	06

Source : Railway and Traffic Wing (203).

Fault of the driver, mechanical fault and the bad road conditions account for 83 per cent of the total accidents taking place in Himachal Pradesh. Besides there is a serious problem of lack of information leading to accidents. Batta (2005) finds that it is as a result of asymmetric information that drivers not knowing the vehicle technology and maintenance condition of the vehicle driven by them; the owners do not know the competence of the drivers; both owners and drivers do not know the condition of the roads and commuters do not have any information on all the three players and the number of services available on a particular route. The outcome is adverse selection with owners in their endeavor to save on wage costs select an ill trained person as driver, the drivers drive ill maintained vehicles on roads for want of adequate know how, and the commuters tend to overload such vehicles in search for low fares and for want of adequate information on the consequences. The outcome is almost 100 percent chances of accident. The findings of the study are then compared with the findings of the accident enquiries conducted by the government agencies for accidents taking place on these roods and it clearly emerges that the lack of complete information and combination of adverse selection by all the players had caused four out of five accidents. Thus over 80 per cent of accidents could be avoided just by improving the availability of information to all the players. This heavy incidence of accidents and fatalities making road accidents as one of the major causes of death and disability, make the transportation system unsustainable justifying an urgent policy intervention.

(d) Traffic Congestion

Traffic congestion is described as the situation that arises when the transport networks are loaded with traffic more than its economic capacity (Reddy et.al 2000). The level of traffic congestion in urban transport networks is found to vary with time of the day attaining the maximum level during the peak hours when the journeys to the working places occur. Besides causing delay and enhanced emissions, congestion is responsible for enhanced out of pocket expenses and consequent economic losses. As per a study by Reddy et.al (2000) depending upon the vehicle type, the vehicle operating cost is found to vary from 1.2 to 2.8 times with the fall of speeds from 40 kmph to 10 kmph.

The high growth rates of vehicle population in the state are causing a serious concern in terms of parking spaces and congestion. As the tourist season touches its peak, the regulatory system often collapses in most of the tourist towns due to higher number of vehicles coming from outside. With the parking facilities being insufficient, most of these vehicles are parked on the roads, which further aggravates the problem of traffic management with the road space shrinking due to roadside parking. The problem of traffic congestion reaches its peak during tourist session. The tourism industry in the state has grown significantly in the 1990s. It is estimated on an average about 0.4 to 0.5 million tourists visit the state every year which is equal to about two third of its population (Batta 2003). Major places of attraction are Kullu-Manali, Shimla, Dharamshala-Palampur and Dalhousie-Chamba areas. Tourist season in the state is for almost nine months in a year during which about 0.2 million vehicles registered outside the state enter the state. Finding the existing machinery incapable to handle the situation, the High Court of the state has recently set up a high-powered committee to recommend steps to solve the problem of traffic congestion.

Both liberalization and the carrying capacity of our infrastructure especially roads need to be balanced. As per a recent study done by the Transport Department of Himachal Pradesh (DOT 2003), the capacity of the roads to absorb further traffic is limited. The study calculated the frequency of bus services on important National Highways and found that there was a bus service available on the main National Highways every 1.5 minutes during the peak hours ranging between 7 AM to 7 PM. The average road width on National Highways is 2.5 meters which further goes down in towns falling on the National Highways. In addition to the buses plying on such a small gap, there are other kinds of vehicles on the roads like trucks, government vehicles and the private vehicles. Since most of the National Highways connect important destinations on the tourist circuits, there is a very heavy influx of vehicles during the tourist season spanning for almost nine months in a year. Therefore, these roads are fully saturated and have no capacity to absorb any more traffic.

(e) Environmental Concerns of the Road Transport

The major environmental impact related to the motorised transport is due to the emission of pollutants from vehicle exhausts. It is important to distinguish between local air pollutants, such as carbon monoxide, nitrogen oxides, particles and hydrocarbons, and greenhouse gases, mainly carbon dioxide, nitrous oxide and methane. From the point of view of most countries like India, the most serious environmental impact is that of air pollution, particularly because of its effects on human health. Pollutant emissions from motor vehicles depend on the type of fuel, the vehicle operating conditions and the intensity of the human health impacts from these emissions is a function of the level of exposure. Many people in developing countries, because of lifestyle, economic condition, and occupation, spend large amounts of time in close proximity to road traffic and so are more exposed to harmful emissions. The problem is further aggravated by traffic congestion. Traffic congestion reduces travel speeds and in turn leads to environmental and economic problems because the traffic is congested with a mix of pedestrians and a wide variety of traffic modes. As a result, fuel consumption increases and so are the vehicle emissions, which further exacerbates air pollution and increases the noise levels.

Table 8.10 : Health and Ecological Effects of Air Pollution

Pollutants	*Effects on Human Health*	*Effects on Natural Environment*
Carbon monoxide (CO)	Can affect the cardiovascular system, exacerbating cardiovascular disease symptoms, particularly angina: may also particularly affect fetuses, stickle cell anaemies and young children; can affect the central nervous system, impairing physical coordination, vision and judgment, creating nausea and headaches, reducing worker productivity and increasing personal discomfort.	
Nitrogen oxides (NO)	Nitrogen dioxide (NO_2) can affect the respiratory system: Nitrogen monoxide (NO) and Nitrogen dioxide (NO_2), where they play a part in photochemical smog formation, may indirectly increase susceptibility to infections, pulmonary diseases, impairment of lung function and eye, nose and throat irritations.	NO and NO_2 can contribute significantly to acid deposition, damaging aquatic ecosystems and other ecosystems such as forest; NO can also have a fertilizing effect on forests.
Sulphur oxides (SO)	Sulphur dioxide (SO_2) can affect lung function	Sulphur oxides can contribute significantly to acid deposition impairing aquatic and forest ecosystems. Sulphates can affect the perception of the environment by reducing visibility eve at low concentrations.
Particular mater (SPM and PM 10	Fine particulars matter may be toxic in itself or may carry toxic (including carcinogenic) trace substances, and can alter the immune system. Fine particulates can penetrate deep into the	Fine aprticulates can significantly reduce visibility. High dust and soot levels are

	particulates can penetrate deep into the respiratoy system thus irritating lung tissues and causing long-term disorders.	of dirtiness of the environment
Lead	Can cause brain damage, encephalopathy in children resulting in lower IQ, death, hyperactivity and reduced ability to concentrate.	

Source : Houghton and Hunter (1994).

Among the sectors of the economy that account for CO_2 emissions from energy, prominent are fuel combustion in industry (41 percent), electricity production (34 percent) and transport (17 percent). Within the transport sector, it is estimated that two wheelers and cars contribute to 78 per cent and 11 percent respectively of vehicular pollution. Three wheelers contribute around 5 percent, buses 2 percent and trucks 4 percent (Patankar 2000). Among the principle factors that determine vehicular emissions (Reddy 2000) are engine technology, vehicle mass, fuel quality, maintenance and aerodynamic drag. In Himachal Pradesh two factors contribute mainly to the vehicular pollution namely a large population of two wheelers and rising population of diesel vehicles. Apart from their higher population leading to higher emissions (over two third of the total population are two wheelers), most of the Indian two wheelers are intrinsically polluting because of their design because of the short-circuiting of the charge out of exhaust without being burnt in the engine and the lubricating oil being exhausted with the short-circuited charge. In addition, the two stroke engines tend to wear faster than the four-stroke engine and their spark plugs tend to get fouled very frequently leading to further emissions.

Second, the rising population of diesel engines is also a cause of concern. The situation is further complicated due to the fact that the diesel sold in India has higher sulfur content (Patankar 2000) and as the diesel engines emit more black smoke full of suspended particulate matter if the engines are not properly maintained, the often poor maintenance and absence of life span of the vehicle adds fuel to the fire.

On the issue of environmental externalities also the situation is no way better. Owing to its geo-physical features (mountainous area and location on the Himalayas), the ecosystems here are more sensitive to environmental damage (S&T 2000). The State Pollution Control Board has set up monitoring stations at major industrial and tourist towns in the state. As per its latest report (PCB 2003), the ambient air quality in major tourist and industrial towns is deteriorating with SPM, NOx and PM_{10} reaching threshold levels.

8.5 Agenda for Reform

(i) Re-orienting Motor Vehicle Taxation

As a closer look at the policy regime in the transport sector in India reveals that there is a clear-cut division of responsibilities between the federal and the state governments. The Motor Vehicles Act (which is uniform all over the country) is in the domain of the Government of India while the motor vehicles taxation is a state subject. However, in the current scenario, both do not move in tandem. While the provisions of the Act are framed keeping in view the Government of India's over all strategy on economic reforms, the same is often not reflected in the motor vehicles taxation in the states. The latter is mostly guided by the state's requirements of resource generation. Therefore, the taxation policy may either not reflect the priorities laid down under the Act or may have a tax structure which runs contrary to the overall priorities. For example, while the Act emphasizes on liberalisation and privatisation in the transport sector in India, it is not uncommon to find taxation policies in the states which discourage private investment by keeping tax for the private operators much higher than their public sector counter parts. Most states do not offer a level playing field for the private sector and there is no institution like a regulator in any state in India to ensure a fair competition. Further, even the fare and freight rates in most of the states are fixed by the provincial governments, which for obvious political considerations do not want to charge fares that reflect true cost of operation. While the public sector companies are able to afford such a fare structure due to financial support available from the government budgets, it is difficult for the private operators to survive. As per a rough estimate (DOT 2003), the problem of default in payments of the financial institutions by the private operators is rising in the state. Besides, while the Act provides for All India Tourist Permits and National permits to encourage trade and tourism between the states and envisages a uniform composite taxation for the whole country, most of the states do not follow that. Instead, they have their own tax structure with very is high rates of taxation.

There are contradictions in other areas too. For example, while the Act discourages vehicles with higher pollution emissions, the taxation policy has provisions that run counter to this objective. For instance, charging one time and lower rates of taxes from the personalized vehicles that cause pollution and congestion, and higher annual taxes from the public transport vehicles. Such a taxation policy therefore promotes more private vehicles at the cost of public transport vehicles. Further, within the tax rates for the public transport services, the incidence of tax is very high among luxury vehicles. While the strategy for reduction of private vehicles should be to encourage luxury vehicles to attract more and more commuters to the public transport, the high rates of taxes on luxury and air conditioned buses (which are 100 to 200 per cent more than the ordinary buses), act as a strong deterrent. Therefore, the taxation policy does little to solve the problem of congestion.

There is, therefore, a need to introduce a taxation policy that caters to the transport policy needs: tackling the problems of congestion, road safety and environmental emissions. It is often argued (Mayeres 2003) that taxes on vehicle ownership are not suited to control congestion since they are not related to vehicle use. Likewise, even the taxes on fuel also do little to control congestion since they do not allow differentiation according to time and place of travel. Moreover, the fuel taxes can be avoided by switching to alternate modes of fuel like LPG and electricity (Parrry and Small 2001). Subsidizing travel in public sector is also one alternative often recommended in such situations.

However, a major limitation with this is that it is not possible to use it beyond a point as subsidizing limitlessly may result in other macro economic problems and distortions. A review of literature in transport economics shows that the problem of congestion could be best attended to by a kind of road pricing. Among the easier alternatives of road prices are pay lanes, area licensing and cordon pricing.

Having a differential taxation policy based on age of the vehicles may prove to be useful from the point of view of road safety as well. To discourage older vehicles the taxes on old vehicles should be higher than the new vehicles. Besides, to discourage usage, higher insurance pricing would also reduce excessive use.

(ii) Environmental Externalities

Air pollution in transport is a typical case of negative externality. From a vehicle owner perspective, the marginal benefits of emitting pollutants into the atmosphere, a public good, are more than the marginal costs that he has to bear. In the absence of any intervention the market failure, the social marginal costs will be higher than the private marginal benefits.

The text book solution to the problem is to impose a tax equal to the difference between the private marginal benefits and the social marginal costs. A polluter exposed to such a tax would then internalize the costs of pollution and would take steps to reduce emissions. However, in order to levy such a tax the regulator will require to know the exact pollution caused by each vehicle, which may be difficult especially because the source is mobile, and in a large number. Therefore, the second best solution often recommended in this case is to impose a tax on the polluting goods such as fuel in this case. Higher fuel prices would reduce the vehicle use, reduce the vehicle ownership and encourage the design of more fuel-efficient cars. However, it is often argued (Pandey 2000) that such a tax on the polluting goods has two limitations. First, is related to the failure of the tax to effectively stimulate other initiatives that may for more effective like the technological options. Second, its effect of discouraging the use of the polluting good equally for all the polluters who may have different marginal emission rates.

Eskeland (1994) has shown that in the absence of continuous monitoring of emissions, an effective program aimed at emission reduction will utilize a combination of two instruments which induce better technology and reduce vehicle trips. However, which combination is used depends on the elasticity of demand for the polluting good and the relative cost options. In the context of transport, the reduction of emission will be provided mostly by technical changes if the vehicle fleet is old and poorly maintained and fuel quality is inferior. Conversely, if the vehicle fleet is relatively modern and fuel is of better quality, fuel tax will have a relatively greater role in effecting vehicular emission reduction.

Looking at its impact on pollution reveals that as the token tax is charged on an advalorum basis, vehicles using better technology and thus emitting less pollutants cost more and pay more tax compared to the cheaper vehicles emitting more pollutants. Other examples of similar kind of policy failure could be seen in two stroke versus four stroke engines in two wheelers and Euro II compliant cars versus ordinary cars where the tax rates based on the price of the vehicle act as a strong disincentive for any prospective buyer preferring to buy a cheap more polluting vehicle than the costly less polluting vehicle.

In the case of environmental externalities, the outcome of taxes may be different. For instance, in this case both fuel tax and ownership tax could play a major role in controlling pollution. Since CO_2 emissions are directly related to fuel consumption, fuel tax can be differentiated according to fuel used and its quality though it can not make any distinction between vehicle type for which a tax on ownership may be essential. Taxes on vehicle can play a role, as they can be differentiated according to vehicle type for example, a public service vehicle or a private vehicle. A tax on ownership is simple to implement and generates revenue for the governments. A study by Fullerton and West (2000) shows that a tax on ownership based on the car characteristics like engine size, vintage and the pollution abatement technology applied could provide maximum welfare gain.

(iii) Promoting Safe Transport

Another important externality resulting out of transport use is the impact of the users on accident risks via their level of care reflected in the shape of their driving style and speed and their activity level reflected in the form of number of kilometers traveled. It is argued (Mayeres 2003) that reducing accident externalities rely on the use of liability and compensation rules. The Indian Motor Vehicles Act makes third party insurance necessary for all vehicles. With risk aversion, insurance comes into play. In the Indian circumstances, the insurance premia are not assessed as per individual risk probabilities and instead provide a free riding facility for the relatively risk prone individuals. The premium that one has to pay is not related to the number of kilometers traveled by the insured and the driving habits of the individual. A thorough review of the insurance procedures may be warranted to appropriately price the risk. However, in the absence of a differentiated premia, a kilometer tax or road pricing differentiated as per vehicle type could play a major role.

In terms of compensation, it may be interesting to study the provisions of the Act and their implications. Singh (2004) examines the issue in detail in the Indian context. Singh (2004) argues that economic analysis deals with the important question of whether and how much damage payments are to be made by the injurer to the victims. The measure of the damages paid by the injurer can be considered in two respects: it influences the incentive for the injurer to take optimal care, and it determines as to who should bear the risk of an accident. The efficiency concerns require (Arlen 2000) that the damage compensation should be exactly equal to the harm to force the injurer to take efficient care. The literature on liability rule shows (Jain and Singh 2002) that when both parties can affect the chances of accident, the rule of negligence, the rule of negligence with the defense of contributory negligence, and the rule of strict liability with defense of contributory negligence are efficient. In the Indian context, Singh (2004) evaluates the working of law of torts in motor vehicles context and concludes that it suffers from two types of inefficiencies. First, in many cases due to the court errors, the liability payments are restricted to an amount less than the actual harm making the injurer to not to take efficient care. Second, uncertainties in the assessment of damage reduce chances of out of court settlement and increase litigation.

In addition, the road users also cause damage to the roads, which in turn becomes a cause of accident for the other users. Therefore, a tax on the damage caused could also be useful in controlling road accidents while at the same time providing a resource base to repair the damage. In this case, the road damage is a function of the vehicle weight. The latter depends on the weight per axle. Introduction of a kilometer charge that is a function of the number of axle loads of a heavy vehicle could be an efficient alternative to tackle such a situation.

(iv) Alternative Technologies

With ever depleting supplies of crude oil and rising prices, it is being increasingly felt that alternate modes of transport and alternative sources of fuel for transport related usage needs to be found out. In addition, energy efficient modes of transport like electric trolley; buses and battery-operated vehicles would present a radically different direction in the years to come. A shift from personalized transport to the public transport would also ease the problems of energy consumption, emissions, congestion, and road safety.

It has been advocated that the development of new communication technologies, such as telecommuting, tele-shopping and videoconferencing may allow to limit vehicle use. Concerns include the fact that the available time made possible by such technologies can be used for other (non-business) trips and that activities such as videoconferencing may generate additional travel as a complementary activity. The experience of the telephone as a substitute to the mail system constitute a precedent.

Introduction of mixed traffic modes is yet another factor that could play a major role in reducing emission and improving public safety. Non-motorised vehicles (NMVs) like bicycles, cycle rickshaws and carts play an important role in urban transport in many Asian cities accounting for 23 to 30 per cent of vehicle trips in these cities (Patankar 2000). Though the ownership of such vehicles is growing in India along with the other vehicles, however, these face a serious threat of being crowded out of the roads due to the rising numbers of the motorized vehicles. It is often argued that modernization should not be confused with mechanization. The transport planning should invariably include walking and cycling. This integration can be achieved by providing extensive cycle tracks, bicycle parking at important places like market areas, railway stations and educational institutions.

(v) Integration of Transport in Town and Country Planning

An effective transport planning has to begin at the time of planning of a town or a facility. The sustainability of the urban transport system must be considered a critical part of the sustainability of the total urban system. Very often towns, market complexes, and industrial areas are planned without taking into consideration the transport requirements. As a result not enough provisions are made for parking. Many have observed that traffic may eventually expand to fill the road space available. Moreover, new developments around the new roads would cause an increase in the vehicle fleet and in the level of car use. Another way of tackling the problem is by spatially locating trips destinations in a way that optimizes road use. The historical configuration of many urban areas limits the scope of this solution. Moreover, land use and transport are linked by very complex relationships. In general, these constitute longer-term solutions and are characterized by high level of inflexibility. The modification of the natural landscape could be irreversible and the cost of environmental degradation should be taken into account. To protect the built and natural environments, the plan should help reduce car traffic by making public transport an attractive option. Achieving such integration will require coordinated planning of services and facilities; pricing and investment regimes that reflect the full costs and benefits of the various transport modes and close linkage of transport with economic, environmental and social policy initiatives.

8.6 Conclusion

It can be concluded from the discussions above that there is a strong interface between the road development and transport development in an economy. Roads are a necessary infrastructure for development of transportation facility which is turn is important for the growth of an economy. Inadequacy of the road infrastructure often results in problems of congestion, pollution and road accidents, besides being anti-poor. A strategy for roads must therefore encompass traffic management and demand management as well as provision of maintenance of road infrastructure. In a nutshell, the strategy has therefore to include planning and reservation of space for transportation infrastructure, introduce sound maintenance management systems which are supported by sustainable flow of resources, appropriate traffic management systems and the demand management systems which are based on full cost realization. Creation of an agency to coordinate and oversee the working of the system may also be highly useful.

The levels and structure of road taxes have evolved without any underlying economic rationale or specific objectives other than revenue generation. The present tax structure provides neither economic efficiency nor equity. The absence of a national road user charge policy has contributed to multiplicity of taxes and the pricing distortions. A closer look at the policy regime in the transport sector in India reveals that there is a clear-cut division of responsibilities between the federal and the state governments. The Motor Vehicles Act, which is uniform all over the country, is in the domain of the Government of India while the motor vehicles taxation is the state subject. However, very often both do not move in tandem. While the provisions of the Act are framed keeping in view the Government of India's over all policy on economic reforms (Liberalization, Privatization and globalization), the same is often not reflected in the motor vehicles taxation in the states. The latter is often guided by the state's requirements of resource generation. Therefore, the taxation policy may either not reflect the priorities laid down under the Act or may have a tax structure which runs counter to the overall priorities. While tax competition has recently been an area of keen research internationally, enough work has not been done in this area in India. The phenomenon that has been seriously affecting the India automobile industry has unfortunately not been understood properly, especially with reference to its effects on demand for automobiles in different passenger as well as freight segments.

9

E-GOVERNANCE A TOOL FOR CHANGE MANAGEMENT IN TRANSPORT: A CASE STUDY FROM HIMACHAL PRADESH

9.1 Introduction

One of the important reasons for red tape and lengthy procedures in public delivery systems of developing countries including India is our inability to leverage technology. The administrative systems in activities having public interface like the transport management, being documentation intensive, require positive reforms measures to improve image, efficiency and effectiveness of the transport departments. The positive reform measures require involving government policies, government employees, technological innovations, citizen participation and re-engineering of processes. It is estimated (ASRTU 2005) that transport departments in India handle records relating to 41 million vehicles, 50 million driving licenses, investigate 0.2 million accidents and 80, 000 fatalities in a year. The current system of manual maintenance of record is inefficient, prone to rent seeking, and generates information asymmetries in the market. Full automation is therefore recommended to get rid of the system of touts and agents (ASRTU 2005).

E-governance offers an opportunity to use Information and Communication Technology (ICT) for providing better services. Its ability to improve interaction between government and citizens by simplifying procedures, increasing transparency and promoting participatory decision making is especially useful in bringing change management. Among the key objectives that are normally set for e governance initiatives are providing access to information, making transition from passive information access to active citizen participation, and making system more efficient. It is a tool that has the potential of brining in change management. Change management is defined as the plan and implementation of programmes designed to bring about managerial and process changes. The goal of change management is to change behaviour, particularly problem behaviours (Andreasen 1995).

In Himachal Pradesh, the Transport Department's activities are primarily governed by the Motor Vehicles Act, 1988, supplemented by the State's directive and guidelines which are covered by the Himachal Pradesh (HP) Motor Vehicle Rules. As issuance of registration certificates, grant of driving licenses and permits for commercial vehicles by one State has an impact across the country, the Ministry of Road Transport and Highways (MORTH) and Department of Information Technology (DIT), Government Of India felt that all licenses and other permits issued by any state should be made interoperable across the country. Hence, DIT sanctioned pilot projects on e governance to some states of the Indian union and initiated the process of change management in the transport sector. For Himachal Pradesh a pilot project was sanctioned for US $ 2,88,000. Starting from 1st April, 2004, the project covered one of the districts of the state namely the Kangra District. All Registering and Licensing Authorities (RLAs) and the Regional Transport Officer (RTO) Kangra were to be computerized along with the office of Secretary, State Transport Authority (STA) Shimla and the Directorate of Transport Shimla. The first phase was to cover all RLAs and the second phase was to cover the RTO, STA and the Directorate Offices. The fist phase was completed on 31st March 2005 and the second and final phase ended on 31.3.06. The project envisaged studying the present system of working in the transport offices and preparation of an 'As Is' assessment report. Based on the 'As Is' assessment, reform measures were to be identified and implemented. The process of implementation under the project was to be supervised by a state level E-Governance Committee (hereinafter referred to as The Committee) headed by the Principal Secretary of the Transport Department with representatives from Department of Information Technology Government of India and State Government. The day to day management of the project was looked after by the Additional Director Transport who also functioned as the State Level Project Champion for rolling out the initiative in the rest of the state.

The "As Is" assessment report on the functioning of the department revealed that the working in the department was highly individual centric (there was no uniform procedure), had no interface with the stakeholders, without defined objectives and priorities, and had no management information system. The chapter highlights as to how the transport department used the e-governance opportunity to bring in change management. In the exercise the department could simplify procedures, introduce citizen centric working agenda, plug loopholes in taxation, develop management information packages and institutionalize exchange with the stakeholders. The net result of the initiatives taken under the pilot project was improved delivery system, increased revenue collection (receipts increased by 40 percent), and target oriented work culture (the department could achieve all the targets set under transport policy within one year), and more motivated work force.

This chapter is organized as follows. Part-II presents the conceptual framework on e-governance. Along with defining the concept, the various dimensions of the concept are explored. The study uses the Gartner model to evaluate the work done on e-governance in the transport department. Methodology of execution of work under the e-governance initiative is also described. Part-III presents the pre-project scenario and the findings of As Is study report. Major initiatives taken under the project are described and results of the initiative are discussed. Part-IV gives the road map for future and conclusions and recommendations.

II

9.2. Conceptual Framework

E-governance is defined as the application of electronic means in the interaction between government and citizens and government and businesses, as well as in internal government operations to simplify and improve democratic, government and business aspects of Governance (Backus 2001). The fulfillment of this objective will require changes in internally focused processes (operations) and externally focused services. The external objective of e-governance is to satisfactorily fulfill the public's needs and expectations on the front-office side, by simplifying their interaction with various online services. The use of ICTs in government operations facilitates speedy, transparent, accountable, efficient and effective interaction with the public, citizens, business and other agencies.

In the back-office, (internal strategic objective) the objective of e-governance in government operations is to facilitate a speedy, transparent, accountable, efficient and effective process for performing government administration activities. Significant cost savings (per transaction) in government operations can be the result. Any e-governance initiatives focuses on three main target groups: government, citizens and business/interest groups. The external strategic objective focus on citizens, businesses and interest groups; the internal objectives focus on government itself. The most common group interactions are presented in figure-7.

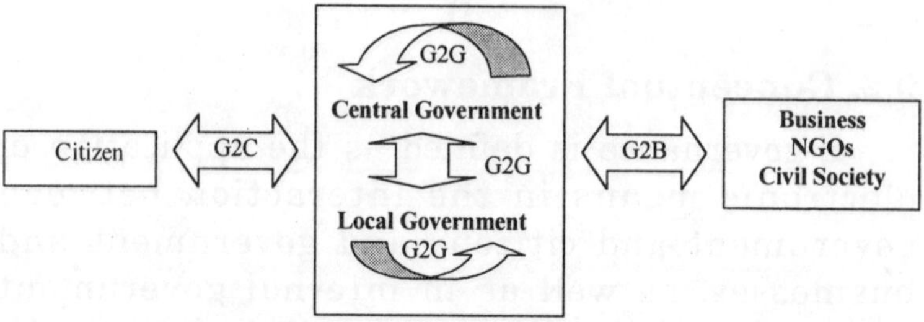

Figure 7: Interaction between main groups in e-governance (Backus 2001)

G to C is government to citizen, G to B is government to business and G to G is government to government.

"Gartner (2000) has formulated four phase e-governance model. According to Gartner the e-governance model can serve as a reference for governments to position where a project fits in the overall evolution of an e-governance strategy (Figure-8).

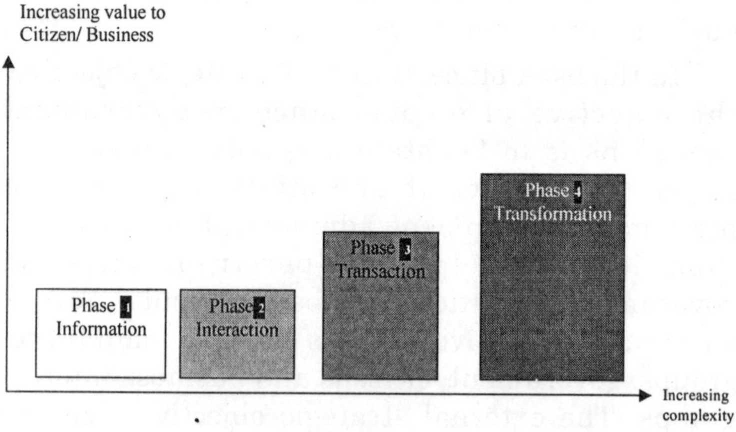

Figure 8: E-Governance Maturity Model (Gartner 2000)

Phase I is information. It basically implies being present on the web, providing external public (G2C and G2B) with relevant information. The format of the first government websites is similar to that of a brochure or leaflet. The value to the public is that government information is publicly accessible; processes are described and thus become more transparent, which improves democracy and service. Internally (G2G) the government can also disseminate information with static electronic means, such as the Internet. This phase it is all about information: from a 1-page presence website to a site with all relevant government information available to the public, in order to improve transparency in democracy.

In the second phase the interaction between government and the public (G2C and G2B) is stimulated with various applications. People can ask questions via e-mail, use search engines for information and are able to download all sorts of forms and documents. These functionalities same time. In fact the complete intake of (simple) applications can be done online 24/7. Normally this would have only been possible at a counter during opening hours.

Internally (G2G) government organizations use Local Area Networks (LAN), intranets and e-mail to communicate and exchange data. The bottom line is that more efficiency and effectiveness is achieved because a large part of the intake process is done online. However, one still needs to go to the office to finalize the transaction, by paying a fee, handing over evidence or signing papers. The use of electronic communications tools speed up the internal government processes.

With phase three the complexity of the technology increases, but customer (G2C and G2B) value will also be higher. Complete transactions can be done without going to an office. Examples of online services are filing income tax, filing property tax, extending/renewal of licenses, and visa and passports. Phase three is mainly complex because of security and personalization issues for example digital (electronic) signatures are necessary to enable legal transfer of services. Internal (G2G) process have to be redesigned to provide good service. Government needs to create new laws and legislation that will enable paperless transactions with legal certification.

The fourth phase is the transformation phase in which all information systems are integrated and the public can get G2C and G2B services at one (virtual) counter. One single point of contact for all services is the ultimate goal. The complex aspect in reaching this goal is mainly on the internal side, for example the necessity to drastically change culture, processes and responsibilities within the government institution (G2G). Government employees in different departments have to work together in a smooth and seamless way. In this phase cost savings, efficiency and customer satisfaction are reaching highest possible levels.

The above four phases lead to a total transformation in the work culture of the organization. Before going for a change in the existing system the stakeholders have to be clear about *what, why and how* are they planning for a change. The change management thus becomes a matter how members of the public service make the transition form the traditional approaches to an era of management through ICT.

Table 9.1: Overview e-governance solutions for each phase

Overview e-governance solutions			
	External : G2C	**External: G2B**	**Internal: G2G**
Phase 1 Information	Mission statements, Addresses, opening hours, employees, telephone numbers Laws, rules and regulations Petitions Government glossary News	Business information Addresses, opening hours, employees, telephone numbers Laws, rules and regulations	Knowledge base (static intranet) Knowledge management (LAN)
Phase 2 Interaction	Downloading forms on websites Submitting forms online help with filling in forms (permits, birth/death certificates) Intake processes for permits, E-mail, Newsletters, Notification	Downloading forms on websites Submitting forms Online help with filling in forms (permits) Intake processes for permits E-mail Notification	E-mail Interactive knowledge databases Complaint handling tools
Phase 3 Transaction	License applications/renewals Renewing car tags, vehicle registration Personal accounts (mytax, myfines, mylicenses etc.) Payment of taxes Registering online	License applications and renewals via website Payment of taxes Procurement	Inter-governmental transactions
Phase 4 Transformation	Personalized website with integrated personal account for all services	Personalized website with integrated business account for all services	Database integration

9.3. Methodology

All transport activities in the state are handled by the Regional Transport Officers (RTOs) located at the ten of the twelve districts of the state and Registering and Licensing Authorities (RLAs) operating at the Sub Divisional level. The division of work between RTOs and RLAs is that while RTOs mostly handle grant of permits and collection of taxes, the RLAs issue driving licenses and register vehicles. Inspection of vehicles for mechanical fitness is done by a Board of Inspection consisting of RLAs and the Motor Vehicle Inspectors (MVIs). Besides handling the work of registration and grant of licenses and permits, the officers of the department also license and inspect the Pollution Under Control centers (PUC Centers), traders dealing in sale of vehicles, Driving Training Schools and Authorized Testing Stations spread in different parts of the state. The working of the RTO and RLA offices is overseen and coordinated by the Directorate of Transport which is headed by a Director assisted by an Additional and a Joint Director. The Director in turn reports to the Principal Secretary of Transport in Ministry of Transport in the state Government.

The process of change management was started with a study conducted by a team of officers lead by the Additional Director. The team studied the functioning of RTO offices at Shimla and Kangra, RLA offices at Kangra and Dharamshala and the Directorate of transport. The study focused on review of all enactments, rules and procedures, applications formats and grant letters, and conducted a work flow analysis to reduce channels. The whole process right from making an application till the final grant was analysed and the system of maintenance of record was evaluated. At the Directorate level, monitoring systems and the MIS systems were evaluated to find out their exhaustiveness and efficacy. During the study, interviews of stakeholders (operators, staff, public representatives and citizens) were conducted at various places and an incognito exercise of obtaining permits and licenses was also completed. Emphasis during the study was to analyze the system of working, study the attitudes of the functionaries towards computerization and cultural change and find out loopholes for improvement in procedures.

The findings of the assessment were presented before the State level e-governance committee which after detailed deliberations finalized the action plan. The action plan included amending the Motor Vehicles Act and Rules, taxation laws, revision of application and grant performa to include new fields to cater to the Management Information System requirements, drafting a Transport Policy and a Citizen Charter, developing software applications for all activities, launching a web site, institutionalizing consultation with stakeholders and developing a post project sustainability model. All these activities were undertaken and completed in a phased manner after due consultation with the stakeholders.

III

9.4. The Pre-Project Scenario

The findings of the "As Is Assessment Report" summarized the pre-project scenario as under.

(a) Working Environment in Offices

The working environment was characterized by scarcity of space, voluminous record and time consuming procedures. Some interesting observations made in the report were:

- The Department was using obsolete application forms derived from the repealed Motor Vehicles Act of 1939 instead of the currently applicable Act of 1988;
- Records of Token Tax and Registration were not being updated. As a result, vehicles which though had paid taxes were shown in arrears (Accountant General pointed out arrears to the tune of Rs. 63 crore);
- Different practices were being followed in different offices in terms of tax assessment and implementation of Rules. It had resulted in a massive tax leakage;
- There was no system of collection of data and monitoring performance;
- Applicants were required to interact 5 times with various officials before an application was decided making the process time consuming. Citizens considered all this running around as harassment by the Department Officials;

- Under the Motor Vehicles Act, permits holders of the commercial vehicles are required to be prescribed conditions in their permits for operation. However, either conditions were not being prescribed (as in the case of Goods Carriage and Private Service Vehicles) or these did not cover the concerns of the department in transport management (in the case of Stage Carriage permits and Contract Carriage permits);
- Changes in the permits were not being updated on files. As a result, there was substantial leakage in tax realization (for instance, modification of routes were not being updated);
- Although tax clearance is one of the pre-requisites, due to lack of coordination, permits of tax defaulters were also being renewed.

Hence, the manual procedures were inefficient and cumbersome. All parties were loosers : citizen had to struggle a lot for getting small things done; operators lacked information and faced sudden recovery notices when discrepancies were detected by the audit; Government lost revenue; and the employees had to work extra hours to finish their work and faced departmental action as short realization of tax was discovered.

(b) No Interface with Operators and No Feed Back Mechanism

The Department functioned in a typical regulatory frame work having absolutely no interface with the operators. The style of working did not conform to that of a service provider. All policy decisions were drafted and finalized in the department and thrust upon the operators. In most cases these did not relate to the reality in the market (for instance, the department imposed a condition that all cabs getting permits after 2003 will not enter Shimla and Manali towns without having any mechanism to enforce the decision). Consulting the stakeholders was considered as derogatory for a regulatory authority. Never ever did the department consult operators or commuters on fixation of fare and freight and time tables. As a result the fare and freight rates fixed by the government were never implemented. Serious mismatch were reported in time tables of buses and the demand for services.

(c) No Consideration of Objectives and Priorities

As the Department had not defined its objectives and priorities, the normal functioning of the Department remained focused on attending to day to day problems and pressures without any consideration for the long term requirements in the Transport sector. For example, route permits for cabs were sanctioned in large numbers even for small towns regardless of demand for such services. Resultantly, most of these were actually operating as stage carriage vehicles carrying passengers and competing with the buses. Enforcement staff was always under pressure to fine them.

(d) No MIS at all

There was no system of monitoring disposal of work in the Department. Surprisingly, even the tax receipts of the Department were also not being monitored. As a result, money received in the form of Bank Drafts from other states was either not being deposited at all or was being deposited after a lapse of many years.

(e) Disjointed functioning (Multiple Islands)

One of the important findings of the 'As is Report' which was later reconfirmed while doing the software customization was that all the offices had their own independent procedures based on precedences or their interpretation of provisions of the Act. This had resulted in every office following different procedures in respect of disposal of matters and levy of tax leading to leakage of money and avoidable inconvenience to the operators. In certain cases, it also came to light that some of the offices were charging certain fees over and above the rates fixed by the Government. Thus the standardization resulting from software development led to reduction of fees in certain cases.

(f) Highly individualistic working approach

As each authority was following its own procedures and charging taxes as per its own interpretation, it had resulted in individual centric working approach in which employees used to decide the outcome of an application making it amenable to whims and fancies. Due to this factor, officials working in the registration and permit seats gained indispensability: in most places the officials had longer tenures doing the same work.

9.5. Initiaves Taken and Milestones Achieved

Among the major initiatives taken under the pilot project included the following.

(a) Revising the Procedures

Revising procedures involved revising the application forms, permit formats, delegation of powers and reducing the channels of processing an application. All application forms were reviewed and redundant columns were substituted with information that would be required for various purposes. Additional information sought under the new columns was total investment in the enterprise, number of people likely to be employed, the family income and employment status of the applicant, gender information and belonging to caste and other preferred categories. All the new areas were identified keeping in view the information requirements of various agencies like government, press, public representatives and the State Legislative Assembly.

Permit formats were revised to include conditions of permit and additional information on vehicles type, mode and area of operation. Powers of issuing National Permits were delegated from the Directorate to the RTOs to reduce delays and provide service at the door step. Likewise, procedures for entertaining applications for PUCs and Traders license were also revised. A guideline booklet containing application forms and procedures was published to facilitate people in understanding the procedures and disseminate information.

(b) Amending Acts and Rules

Probably the most paying exercise from the government's perspective was the review of taxation act and motor vehicle rules. It resulted in identification of areas of leakages and possibilities of levying taxes or fees wherever it was possible. For example, it was noticed that no tax was levied on old vehicles purchased from other states, vehicles being re-registered as a result of change of use (from commercial to private), and on completion of 15 years life. Though as per the provisions of the Act, vehicles were inspected for fitness after 15 years of age but no tax was levied after 15 years of life. Similarly, construction equipment vehicles were also totally out of the tax net. Rates of token tax on tourist vehicles were lower than the passenger vehicles which besides being unfair provided an advantage to the tourist vehicles to offer lower fares than the passenger vehicles and poach into the passenger vehicles segment. The rates of composite fee charged from vehicles entering from other states under the National/All India Permits were very low and with no mechanism of collection. It resulted in loss of revenue and offered undue advantage to the vehicles coming from other states. Taking all the above changes into account, a bill amending the Himachal Pradesh Motor Vehicles Taxation Act was introduced and passed in the state assembly in 2004.

Similar situation prevailed in the fee structure for various services. For example, the counter signature fee charged by the neighbouring states was Rs. 1000 per annum where as Himachal was charging only Rs. 250. Besides, certain fees prescribed under the Central Motor Vehicles Rules were not being charged at all (for example Fee for issuing fitness certificates). Provisions of the H.P. Motor Vehicle Rules 1999 were amended to revise and levy fees.

(c) Defining Objectives though Transport Policy

Transport Policy was notified in August, 2004. The policy aimed at providing mobility with choice, comfort, convenience, frequency, safety and minimal environmental effects. The objective included following initiatives:

- A mechanism for redressal of public grievances and getting a feedback was provided in the form of :
  - a State Transport Development Council to be set up with representation from all the stakeholders; and
  - making it obligatory for the Director to to hold meetings with operators.
- Aimed at generating employment opportunities and improving connectivity, the policy laid down guidelines for grant of permits. Under the policy, a blanket ban on grant of Stage Carriage Permits (passenger buses) was imposed and priority was given to the rural areas only. Weaker sections like

Scheduled Castes and Tribes, ex-servicemen, widows and people living below the poverty line were to be given priority in grant of permits;

- Better tourist facilities were sought to be provided through metered taxis and pre-paid taxis systems. Luxury services were to be promoted;
- Common access facilities like Bus Stands and Parkings are sought to be provided more efficiently and with 15 years perspective;
- For housing workshops, Transport Nagars are sought to be established; and
- Controlling vehicular pollution and improving road safety.

(d) Software and MIS

The AS is report identified following areas as critical areas for development of MIS:

(a) Monitoring of Tax and Non-tax receipts;

(b) Monitoring recovery on arrears of Special Road Tax;

(c) Barrier receipt;

(d) Composite fee receipt and position of Bank Drafts requiring revalidation bank-wise;

(e) Disposal of pending matters of Regional Transport Authorities.

Hence, the software on above were developed and operationalised. Software developed by the National Informatics at the National level named Vahan and Sarthy was customized for catering to the state requirements.

(e) Site Development

One of the key findings of the report was bad condition of offices, in appropriate lay out and poor maintenance of record. The study observed that the poor layout and worn out furniture was affecting the morale of the employees. Thus, as a part of the change management initiative, all offices were renovated with layout plans akin to those in customer oriented agencies like Banks and Insurance Companies. Documents are now being accepted and handed over from a counter instead of the earlier practice of each applicant visiting the officials. In the pre-project scenario, the operators visiting to pay taxes were not even offered a chair and in some places had to stand in the open without a roof overhead. Separate waiting places for visitors were created in all places. A proper meeting hall was constructed in the Directorate.

(f) Meetings and Workshops

The initiative successfully incorporated a provision in the Transport Policy mandating the Director Transport to hold consultations/meetings with the operators and other stakeholders. During the tenure of the project one National level Workshop on Road Safety and Pollution prevention was held while one day workshops were held at ten places covering issues like revision of rates of special road tax, road safety, pollution prevention, AIDs prevention and fixation of fare and freight rates. A culture of stakeholder's consultation and making overhead or power point presentation had evolved in the organization.

(g) Sustainability Model

Another major challenge under the project was making it sustainable. While the initial works could be done out of the project funds, the subsequent recurring expenditure on account of maintenance of buildings, computers, salary of additional manpower required, and other miscellaneous expenditure on printing and stationery was required to be funded. Leaving it to the normal budgetary means would have led to resource gap. Hence, an independent entity in the form of a society under the Society Registration Act 1860 was created with the following mandate:

(a) It was authorized to levy user charges on additional services rendered in the process of computerization. However, since the objective was to boost efficiency and bring cultural change by adopting client oriented approach, it was incorporated in the user charge notification that if the agency failed to deliver documents within the time frame fixed under the citizen charter, the user charge will be required to be refunded;

(b) The agency could employ people on contract basis. However, to ensure that the money is not used in un-productive areas, the society was debarred from spending on travel abroad and purchase of vehicle (norms of financial prudence developed under the project were later circulated by the government for all societies registered prior or after the transport department e-governance society);

(c) No tax or fee could be deposited in the Society funds.

9.6. Outcome of the Initiative

(a) Revenue receipts of the department jumped from Rs. 78 crore in 2003-04 to Rs. 109 crore in 2004-05 (increased by 40 percent). The amendments in tax laws and state rules are fetching Rs. 25 crore per annum additionally;

(b) Working environment changed drastically with every office having new layout, furniture and face lift of building. Each dealing hand got a PC to work on;

(c) Disposal of cases increased with average time consumed reducing from 3 days to 5 hours in most cases;

(d) Initial results revealed that in addition to bringing uniformity of procedures across all RLAs and RTOs, the tax collection and arrear recovery improved substantially with computerized assessment of tax;

(e) The new amendments necessitated tax barriers to be installed at various places. As inconvenience caused to the operators and the cost benefit analysis of opening new offices was highlighted, government approved opening of RTO offices in three more districts. With this staff got promotions and a stage came when the people on the feeder category were not available for filling up the higher positions. It acted as a major motivating factor for the employees;

(f) Resource mobilization under the Society was very encouraging. Along with levying user charges, the Society started printing guidelines booklets, selling space for advertisements, and got a project on AIDs prevention. On an average the society was getting Rs. 5 lakh per month as user charges (which is far more than the routine contingency budget of Rs. 18 lakh per annum that the Department was getting).

IV

9.7. Conclusion

Though the computerization work was successfully completed during the project, there remained some important tasks to be taken up during the roll out period. These are:

(a) While activities having strong interface with public got priority in software development, all the activities undertaken in the RTO offices could not be covered. Therefore, in the roll out plan four activities were identified for software development namely time table of stage carriage buses, RTA business software, software covering miscellaneous services like driving training schools, PUCs and Traders licenses, and computerization of accounts;

(b) Vahan, Sarthi and Permit software need to be rolled out in all RLA and RTO offices. After all offices are covered, the department has to work on interconnectivity and data transferability between the offices to save time and facilitate movement of vehicles between RLAs and RTOs within the outside the state;

(c) With the completion of back end computerization, it will be possible and cost effective to undertake Smart card based licenses and Registration;

(d) Though the department had launched a web site with detailed information, however, web based services like renewal of permits, licenses and deposit of tax is still a far cry. The perspective planning needs to keep this on priority;

(e) The Society has already become functional and has started receiving funds through user charges. In the next phase it should focus on operator oriented services. It should take operators on its executive body to get suggestions on the possible areas of improvement in the delivery of services; and

(f) Finally, the department needs to workout arrangement with banks for accepting taxes and fees directly from the operators all over the state.

The initiative therefore took comprehensive measures to improve working in the Transport Department. Seen in terms of Gartner model, the project had only achieved the first two stages and is ripe to start work on the remaining two stages. The project led change in work culture is so much that a department which used to only think in terms of policing suddenly become a service provider and started focusing on development of services and quality of delivery.

10
CONCLUSION

Without access to jobs, health, education and other amenities, not only the quality of life suffers but with inability to access resources and markets, growth stagnates and poverty reduction cannot be sustained. Studies by the World Bank show that transport generates growth by facilitating trade, both nationally and internationally, and by increasing access to health and education facilities (Easterly and Rebelo 1993). Conversely, inappropriately designed transport strategies and programs can result in networks and services that aggravate the conditions of the poor, harm the environment, ignore the changing needs of users, and cause drain in public finances. In urban areas, the quality of transportation infrastructure and public transport service affects the location decisions made by firms and individuals, the scale and form of urban developments, the efficiency of the labor market and the costs at which labor is obtained.

However, with the transport activities having substantial external effects imposing cost to the society, sustainable transportation is the cornerstone for sustainable development. The objective of sustainability can only be achieved if the economic, environmental and social concerns are addressed. The economic considerations require reducing transport energy costs with inter modal efficient transport networks, stimulate economic growth with safe and affordable transport network for all, and efficient pricing of transportation infrastructure with receipts of pricing allocated for transport infrastructure development. Environmental considerations require more efficient use of non-renewable resources, reducing green house emissions through rational use of transport, promoting zero or low emission public transport and equitable allocation of urban space to more efficient modes. Societal considerations require safe travel and equitable access.

Verhoef (1996) analyses the external costs of transport along two dimensions: as per their impacts and the type of source. In the first category (who is affected) there three possibilities: intra-

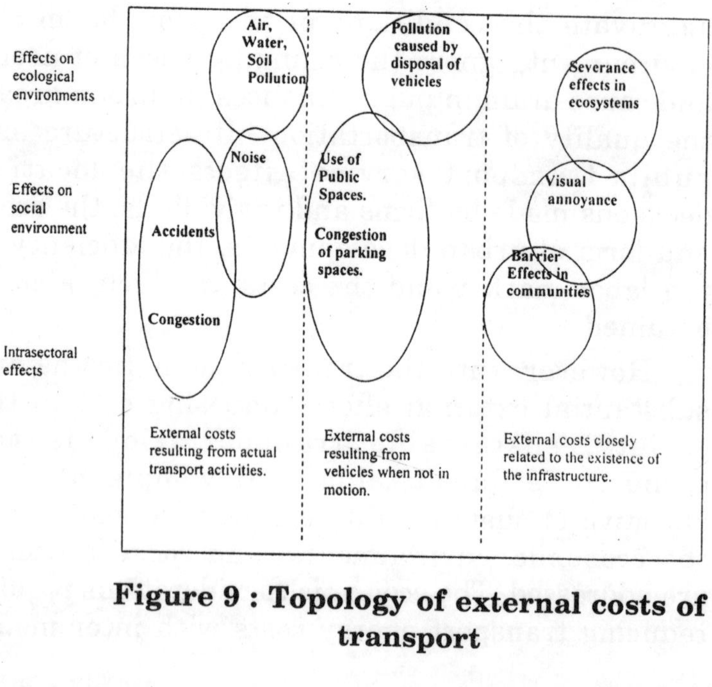

Figure 9 : Topology of external costs of transport

sectoral effects, effects on social environment, and effects on ecological environment. In the second category (type of source) are arising due to vehicle use, when vehicle is not in motion, and the infrastructure related. Figure-1 illustrates these externalities.

By causing congestion the road users impose costs on themselves, accidents cause a cost to the society and pollution causes ecological costs. The external costs also occur when the vehicles are not in use. For example, congestion of parking spaces, use of public spaces, and environmental problems caused due to disposal of vehicles. Transport infrastructure also causes externalities in the form of visual and environmental effects caused by it.

As an integral part of economic policy, it is up to transport policy to establish the general conditions necessary for coping with the freight mobility requirements resulting from economic activity. However, it has no specific remit to control national and international trade, insofar as freight traffic is the consequence of decisions taken outside the transport sector by economic policy makers and manufacturing and commercial firms. The role of transport policy is to put in place the conditions which will ensure greater efficiency of all activities relating to the transport economy. In particular, this means:

- Providing transport infrastructure of a high standard, in terms of both quantity and quality;
- Establishing the necessary conditions for non-discriminatory competition within and between modes;

- Using the same method of calculation to charge infrastructure costs to all transport modes, while still allowing for the possibility of an appropriate contribution from the public exchequer towards the infrastructure development;
- Issuing regulations establishing norms in respect of harmful emissions and noise pollution, vehicle characteristics, etc.

With respect to Himachal Pradesh, remodeling transport policy will help a great deal. A combination of command and control instruments and economic instruments will be the most effective way. Among the main problems that need to be addressed in the road sector in Himachal Pradesh are:

- Insufficient investment in the primary networks vis a vis the demand for road transport;
- Inadequate or suboptimal allocation of resources for road maintenance;
- Absence of private sector participation in road construction and management; and
- Inadequate attention to road safety.

When orderly planning and execution of road maintenance is undermined through insufficient budgetary sources, road networks can deteriorate to the point that production and distribution costs of other economic activities are significantly increased. One of the often recommended solutions to the road problems is creating a road fund. Road funds are a continuing subject of controversy: they are regarded as a boon by the road managers while considered as a bane by the macroeconomists. There are three cardinal principles in the creation and management of road funds. First, the road funds expenditure responsibilities should be limited to maintenance in order to correct a systemic bias against maintenance. Second, road funds revenue should be collected only from direct charges on road users. Finally, the road fund has to be managed professionally under the direction of a user representative body and subject to strict oversight and auditing arrangement of independent auditors.

With respect to road safety, one of the strongest reasons for the government to intervene in the form of a transport policy or a road safety policy is road safety being a 'merit good'. Consumers are not able to assess its utility adequately, or may not have access to information. This may be due to the face that accident is a rare event in the individual's driving career. This problem can be approached on the demand side of the equation by influencing consumer decision making behaviour. On the supply side, production and distribution of potentially dangerous goods can be discouraged or even stopped. Another important reason for the transport policy intervening in this matter is due to the need for a compulsory insurance to cover the third party risks. Compulsory insurance is a potential tool to enable the policy makers to ensure internalization of external costs of driving.

One of the important factors in the insurance costs is that ex ante payment of a compulsory insurance premium does influence other decisions than ex post payment of compensation. A premium is part of the overhead expenses taken into account when deciding on the purchase or use of a vehicle. Probability of an accident and its financial consequences is supposed to be taken into account when deciding on the purchase of a vehicle. From safety viewpoint first form of pricing (ex ante) is preferable to the second (ex post). The more insurance premiums are reflecting risks of accident costs by differentiations based on safety characteristics of a vehicle, the driver and the roads used, the more the costs are internalized.

Any policy to check pollution emanating from the vehicle exhaust has to have four components : relating to the vehicle technology, vintage, fuel used, and usage. Over the years, *vehicle technology* has substantially improved resulting in better fuel efficiency and lesser emissions. Among the petrol driven vehicles, introduction of four stroke engines in two and three wheelers and accurate fuel injection systems controlled by electronics are the most significant from the environmental perspective. The electronic control systems tend to optimize the ignition and the injection requirements. In the diesel engines, there is a trend towards direct injection engines. In the developed, countries the proportion of direct injection vehicles is almost 75 percent of the total diesel vehicles.

While vehicles of the above technology are now being manufactured and sold in India, it is, however, important to develop an arrangement that encourages introduction and use of better technology vehicles. A suitable policy framework is also required to provide incentive to the in-use obsolete technology vehicles to adopt new technology interventions. The road tax or the token tax needs to be so structured that the incidence of the tax reduces with the technological improvements and reduction in pollution emissions and increases with the level of pollution. Suitable tax concessions could be provided for four stroke engines in two and three wheelers, Euro-II engines in petrol and turbo engines in diesel vehicles.

While improvements in technology would certainly enhance performance parameters in pollution and road safety among new vehicles, attention also needs to be given to the in-use vehicles. Among the in-use vehicles, Inspection and Maintenance Program, Manufacturer Warranty Program and Scrape Program could help tackling the problem. As per the provisions of the Motor Vehicles Act 1988, all commercial vehicles have to obtain a certificate of fitness once in a year and private vehicles after 15 years of life and every five years thereafter. It has been done to ensure maintenance of vehicles. Introducing a progressive taxation that increases with the life span of the vehicle could induce early replacement or scrapping by the owners. In addition, incentivising retro fitment of catalytic converters and engine replacements could also bring remarkable results. It is estimated (Reddy 2000) that older commercial vehicles retrofitted with modern engines could reduce particulate levels at least by 80 percent and Hydro Carbons by 60 percent with no increase in NOx and noise levels.

Extending the responsibility of performance to the manufacturer is also one of the often recommended options. Owing to the modest success of the current inspection and maintenance systems, there is a trend to shift the liability of maintaining emission control throughout the life of the vehicle on manufacturers through the warranty coverage requirements on emission control equipment. As the manufacturers would not like to be penalized through the warranty covered repairs, the quality of the equipment will improve. It is being currently achieved by making suitable provisions in the Central Motor Vehicle rules.

Vintage or the age of the vehicle is another important factor affecting the pollution levels. It is important in India since the maximum life span of vehicles has not been prescribed. Modernizing the vehicle fleet by incentivising retirement is an effective option in this regard. As new vehicles are cleaner than older ones, policies that encourage early scrap page of the older vehicles can yield significant emission reduction. One of the options used by many countries is introduction of a subsidy on scrapping a vehicle. The success of scrappage program in terms of cost effectiveness and emission reduction however depends on the amount of subsidy. If the subsidy offered is less than the selling price of the old vehicles, it may not be effective while raising the level of subsidy may reduce cost effectiveness. Besides, due caution has to be maintained to ensure that the subsidy does not reduce incentive to maintain the vehicle.

In terms of *fuel use*, CNG, LPG and petrol are considered to be less polluting compared to leaded petrol and diesel. Introduction of an emission charge based on fuel used is often advocated. A differentiated fee structure based on classifications given at table 1 is recommended to encourage use of environment friendly fuel and technology in vehicles. It could further be made a progressively graduated charge based on the life of the vehicle.

Table 10.1: Motor Vehicle Taxation based on age and fuel used

Sr. No.	*VEHICLE TYPE*	*Rates of tax*			
		10 yrs	*15yrs*	*25yrs*	*Above 25yrs*
1.	**Cars (Petrol)**				
2.	**Cars Diesel**				
3.	**Taxies**				
4.	**Taxies**				
5.	**Three Wheelers (Petrol Two Stroke)**				
6.	**Three Wheelers (Diesel)**				
7.	**Two Wheelers (two stroke)**				
8.	**Two Wheelers (four stroke)**				
9.	**Buses**				

Finally, the *vehicle usage* (private versus commercial) is also an important factor. As the commercial vehicles ply more, they tend to emit more pollutants. Besides, the problems of overloading and bad maintenance are also associated with the commercial vehicles. Therefore, the incentives for technological interventions like catalytic converters, electronic fuel injections, turbo chargers, modern carburetors and conversion to greener fuels need to be built in the emission fee or tax rate structures.

Traffic congestion imposes substantial cost to the society: pollution, energy costs and time costs. With the ever-increasing vehicle population and increasing vehicle miles, the situation on congestion is likely to worsen in future. Consequently, transport planners and policy analysts are faced with the problem of finding a policy tool to handle it. Among the options are road pricing, subsidizing the public transport and introduction of rapid mass transit systems.

One of the options tried in many places of the world is road pricing. Economists have advocated it as an effective way of allocating scarce roadway capacity to the highest valued users. Among the most popular types of the road pricing are pay lanes, area licensing and cordon pricing. With *pay lanes*, of which the high occupancy or toll lanes are the examples, one of the several highway lanes is tolled while the others are not. The system seeks to improve efficiency by sorting drivers according to their value of time. The *area licensing* requires a license to drive in certain areas. Examples of its use are found in Singapore and several European countries. The *cordon pricing* aims at reducing congestion through a differentiated charge for entry into the area within the cordon. Well known examples of cordon pricing are found in Norwegian cities and in London.

One of the best examples of the road pricing is the congestion charge of London. At five pounds per day the charge currently raises about 500000 pounds per day. It is estimated that due to this charge traffic is reduced by at least 20 percent. Besides, the money so raised is spent on improvement of bus services in the London city. However, congestion pricing has at least three major limitations : high implementation costs, privacy issues and distributional effects. High implementation costs arise as a result of the need for a barrier to collect the toll. With manual collections, the costs and time implications both rise. However, the recent introduction of electronic smart cards to collect the toll has helped a great deal. Privacy issues arise mainly in the manual form of collection and are by and large over come with the smart cards. Distributional effects of congestion tolls remain an area of concern. Since everyone pays the same toll regardless of income, low income motorists suffer disproportionately. Compensating the potential users by appropriately spending the revenue could help in improving the political feasibility of congestion pricing.

Subsidizing the public transport could be achieved in two ways: cash subsidy for operation and tax incentives to the public transport operators. While the first one is considered to be inefficient and also puts strain on the fund-starved governments, the tax concessions have found favour with governments in many countries.

The high-capacity mass transit system needs a serious consideration where very little additional capacity can be squeezed out of the existing system. The latent demand for road use, for example, is so high that any additional space is immediately occupied not only by vehicles in motion but also by parked vehicles particularly the freight vehicles, hawkers, and slums. Making improvements in public transport is an optimal way of responding effectively, at affordable costs and in an energy-efficient and environmentally sustainable manner, to the present and future transportation needs of the vast majority of people in developing countries. It leads to the establishment of integrated transportation systems, made up of complementary transportation modes that are compatible with travel demand and affordable by the urban population.

Ravibabu (2006) presents detailed analysis on investments in alternate systems of Mass transport. As per this, while surface rail system is expected to cost Rs. 8 Crore per kilometer, under ground rail costs Rs. 250 to 300 Crore, elevated rail costs Rs. 150 -180 Crore, and mono rail Rs. 100 to 150 Crore. The capacity of surface and elevated rail systems is comparable (varying between 8000 and 40000 passengers per hour per direction), mono rail has 20 per cent lesser capacity. Patel (2006) offers a similar analysis based on the Bus Rapid Transit Systems. Among the salient features of such a system are buses with wide doors, operating from specially created passenger platforms and plying on the dedicated tracks. BRTs have a capacity to carry 10-20000 passengers per hour per direction at the investment of Rs. 2.50 Crore per kilometer.

Of the above, road pricing continues to be preferred to a fuel tax and higher subsidy on public transport. Studies in use of economic instruments show that equity considerations do not have a large impact on ranking of transport instruments. Moreover, the use of revenue generated through the road pricing becomes a useful tool to reduce inequalities by improving social security transfers or social services network.

The first phase of control of externalities like the ones discussed above involved traditional legal remedies such as emissions standards. Overtime, however, it became clear that traditional regulatory approaches to pollution control were excessively costly in some circumstances (Tietenberg 1995) and incapable of achieving the stipulated goals in others. Failures have been especially common in developing countries, where legal and regulatory institutions are often weak (Murti, James and Mishra 1999). In response to these deficiencies, the second phase of pollution control focused on market-based approaches. In some circumstances, they have substituted for traditional remedies, while in most of the case they have complemented them. However, even the addition of market-based approaches has not fully solved the problem of pollution control. The main difficulties are encountered in designing, implementing, monitoring and enforcing market-based regulations. For a successful application of economic instruments, it is essential to have researched the environmental costs properly, taking into account the special conditions of developing countries and carefully implementing it in a manner that averts possible disruptive effects and negative distributional impacts. It is argued (World Bank 1992) that the user costs are considered in the production of goods automatically if there are secure property rights and the social discount rate does not deviate too much from the private discount rate. However, with high private discount rates and/or open access resources, environmental costs are not taken into account unless forced to do so with incentive systems or command and control regulations. In other words, an intervention that equalizes the private and social discount rates is warranted. A pricing policy that requires the polluter to pay can deal with the problem.

Providing transport services to meet future needs without causing a serious damage to the environment is a major challenge. A sustainable future transportation system will comprise a mixture of many measures. Introduction of combinations of measures, impacting on the demand and supply of transport services requires appropriate planning techniques which can take account of a wide range of transport, energy and environmental issues and options. The ultimate goal of a transport policy should be to use efficiently road space, a common resource facing the proverbial 'tragedy' of over use, and allow users to take into account the true cost of their decisions, so as to lead to a higher social welfare. The equity implication of such a policy can be a powerful tool for poverty alleviation.

It may be appropriate to sum up the discussions on transport externalities in terms of the Pressure, State and Response model (PSR Model). Table 10.2 presents status in terms of PSR model.

Table 10.2 : Transport Externalities in PSR Framework

Pressure	*State*	*Response*
Rising population, urban expansion, increased human settlements, increased economic activity, demand for leisure travel.	Increased demand for transportation services, overloading, inadequacy of bus services.	Development of Road infrastructure, Transport Planning, integrating transport concerns in town and country planning.
Growth in vehicle ownership due to increased per capita incomes.	Congestion, shortage of parking places, increased travel cost and travel time.	Congestion pricing, parking charges, and introduction of vehicle ownership taxes.
Congestion led increased journey time coupled with more vehicles on road and increased mileage covered.	Environmental pollution in terms of higher gas emissions, idle running during congestion,	Incentives for environment friendly fuel use, promoting better technology vehicles, taxes based on environmental character-ristics, scrap page programes to phase out old technology vehicles.
Increased vehicular population leading to inadequate road space.	Road accidents, increased mortality and morbidity,	Incentives for vehicles with more safety features, changes in insurance pricing to load the cost of accident on the defaulters.
Poverty and income inequalities leading to increased demand for public trans-port.	Increased pressure on public transport, concessions based fare structure leading to increased losses among Public Sector Transport Undertakings.	Planning mass rapid transport systems, cross subsidization for shifting the burdens, integrating transport concerns in town and country planning.

The above table clearly establishes the cause and effect relationship and identifies the policy initiative required to remedy the situation. This framework could also be used as an indicator framework that could help in analyzing the outcome of a development for instance the urban expansion, and assist in taking appropriate policy initiatives.

In this book, an attempt has been made to identify the basic elements needed to analyze transport problems. However, implementing the different interventions requires political will, public support and commitment. It is often argued (Winston 2000) that a major problem with the transport policy is that it is shaped by political forces that inhibit constructive change. Therefore, a commonly recommended solution to the problem is to expose the system to market forces by privatizing it. Given the wide variety of measures and technical possibilities, combined with growing seriousness of excessive fuel consumption, congestion and environmental impacts; this challenge can be overcome. It will however, require institutional reform so as to incorporate integrated planning methods and coordinate implementation, development of suitably skilled manpower and, access to substantial financial resources.

Bibliography

1. **Andreasen, A. R (1995)** *Marketing Social Change: Changing Behaviour to Promote Health, Social Development and the Environment.* San Francisco: Jossey Bass Publications.
2. **Arlen, J (2000)** 'Damages' in B Brouckaert and G De Geest (edt), *Encyclopaedia of Law and Economics*, Edward Elgar: Cheltenham.
3. **Arrow, K.J. and M. Kurz (1970)** *Public Investment, the Rate of Return and Optimal Fiscal Policy.* Baltimore: the John Hopkins Press.
4. **Aschauer, D.A (1989)** Does Public Capital Crowd Out Private Capital. Journal of Monetary Economics, Vol. 24, No. 4: 650-74.
5. **Aschauer, D.A (1993)** Public Capital Productivity and Economic Growth. *In Infrastructure and Competitiveness.* Ontario: John Deutsch Institute for Study of Economic Policy.
6. **ASRTU (2005)** Association of Road Transport Undertakings. http://www.asrtu.org/policy issues8.htm
7. **Backus, M (2001)** E-governance and Developing Countries. *IICD Research Report No. 3, April 2001.*
8. **Barro, R.J.(1993)** Government Spending in a Simple Model of Endogenous Growth. Journal of Political Economy, Vol. 98. No. 2: 339-56.

9. **Batta, R.N. (2003)** Tourism's Potential of Financing Conservation Areas: A Study of Kufri –Chail area. *Tourism Recreation Research*, Vol. 28, No.1.: 34-46.
10. **Batta, R.N. (2005)** *Information Asymetries and Road Safety*. Paper presented in the Conference on Driving training and Safety, Edinburgh.
11. **Baumol, W.J and Oates, W.E (1988)** *Economics, Environmental Policy and Quality of Life,* London:.Prentice Hall, Inc.
12. **Baumol, W.J (1982)** Contestable Markets : An uprising in the theory of Industry Structure. American Economic Review, 72 : 1-15.
13. **British Road Federation (1988)** *The Cost of Congestion.* London: British Road Federation.
14. **CBI (1989)** Transport in London, London Task Force Report. *London Confederation of British Industries.*
15. **CIRT (2005)** *Guidelines for a Model Transport Authority of India. Central Institute of Road Transport*, **Pune: CIRT.**
16. **Coase, R.H (1960)** The problem of Social Cost, *Journal of Law Economics,* Vol. 3, Oct. 1960.
17. **Cropper, M.L. and Oates, W.E (1992)** Environmental Economics: A Survey, *Journal of Economic Literature*, Vol. XXX, :.675-740.
18. **Department for International Development, DFID (2003),** Rural Transport Policy, **www.dfid.org**
19. **DETR (2000)** *Transport 2010: the Ten Year Transport plan.* London: Department of Environment, Transport and Regions.

20. **DOT (2003)** *Annual Administrative Report.* Shimla: Department of Transport.
21. **E&S (2003)** *Economic Survey 2003.* Shimla : Department of Economics and Statistics.
22. **Easterly, W. and S. Rebelo (1993)** Fiscal policy and Economic Growth. Journal of monetary Economics, Vol. 32, No. 3 : 417-458.
23. **Eskeland, G.S. (1994)** The Cost and Benefits of an air pollution control strategy for Santiago, Chile, In *Chile: Managing Environmental Problems: Economic Analysis of Selected Issues.* Report No. 13061-CH,. Washington D.C.: The World Bank.
24. **Freeman, A. M III (1985)** Methods for Assessing the Benefits of Environmental Programs. In A.V Kneese and J. L Sweeney edt. *Handbook of Natural Resources and Energy Economics, Vol. 1.* Amsterdam: North Holland.
25. **Friedrich, R and P. Bickel (2001)** *Environmental External Costs of Transport.* Berlin: Springer-Verlag.
26. **Friedrich, R. and P. Bickel (2001)** *Environmental External Costs of Transport.* Berlin: Springer-Verlag.
27. **Fuller, R. and S.E. West (2000)** Tax and Subsidy combination for the Control of Car Pollution. NBER *Working Paper* 7774. NBER Cambridge MA.
28. **Glanville, W.H. and R.J. Smeed (1957)** the basic requirement for the roads of Great Britain. Proceedings of the Conference on the

Highway needs of Great Britain, *Institution of Civil Engineers.*

29. **Goodwin, P (1992)** Review of New Demand Elasticites. Journal of Transport Economics, Vol. 26. No. 2:155-71.

30. **Goodwin, P (2003)** The Economic Cost of Congestion when Road Capacity is Constrained: Lessons from Congestion Charging in London. *Proceedings of 16th International Symposium on Theory and Practice in Transport Economics, Budapest.*

31. **Houghton, G and Hunter Colin (1994)** *Sustainable Cities. Regional Policy and Development Series. London: Jessika Kingsley.*

32. **Jain, S.K. and R. Singh (2002)** Efficient Liability Rules: Complete Characterization, *Journal of Economics,* 75 (2): 105-24.

33. **Jansson, J.O (2003)** Counterfactual Analysis of Urban Transport Development. *Proceedings of 16th International Symposium on Theory and Practice in Transport Economics, Budapest.*

34. **Jeanrenaud, C. (1997)** Economic Instruments for Economic Policy, In C. Jeanrenaud, Edt. *Environmental Policy Between Regulation And Market,* Birkhauser Verlag basel, Switzerland.

35. **Jonas-lee, M.W.(1991)** Altruism and the value of other people's safety. *Journal of Risk and Uncertainty,* Vol. 4. no 1: 147-156.

36. **Karpagam, M (1991)** *Environmental Economics: A Text Book,* New Delhi: Sterling Publishers Private Ltd.

37. **Karshenas, M (1994)** Environment, Technology and Employment: Towards a New Definition of Sustainable Development, *Development and Change*, Vol. 25, No. 4:723-756.

38. **Lindberg, G.(1999)** benevolence ND THE Value of Statistical Life. *Working Paper* CTEK, Barlange.

39. **Litman, T (2003)** *Evaluating Transport Equity. http.vtpi.org*

40. **Litman, T and David Burwell (2003)** Issues in Sustainable Transportation. http// www.vtpi.org

41. **Mayeres, I (2003)** Taxes and Transport Externalities, *Discussion Paper*, Belgium: Center for Economic Studies.

42. **MORTH (2003)** *Urban Transport Policy for India*. New Delhi: Ministry of Surface Transport.

43. **MORTH (2005)** *National Road Policy*. New Delhi: Ministry of Surface Transport.

44. **Murty, M.N., James, A.J., and S. Mishra (1999)** *Economics of Water Pollution*, Oxford University Press, New Delhi.

45. **Narayan, D (2000)** *Voices of the Poor: Can anyone Hear Us?* New York: Oxford University Press.

46. **Oum, T.H., W. G. Waters, and J.S. Yong. (1992)** Concept of Price Elasticities of Transport Demand. Journal of Transport Economics, May 1992: 139-154.

47. **Pandey, R (2000)** *Economic Policy Instruments for Controlling Vehicular Air Pollution*. New Delhi: NIPFP.

48. **Parry, IWH. And K. Small. (2001)** Does Britain or the United State Have the right Gasoline Tax? Washington, DC: Resource for the Future.

49. **Patankar, P.G. (2000)** Urban Transport, *Survey of the Environment, 2000*. New Delhi: The Hindu.

50. **Patel, S.B. (2006)** Advantages of Bus Rapid Transit Systems. *Economic and Political Weekly, May 20, 2006: 2035.*

51. **PCB (2003)** Status of the Environment in Himachal Pradesh. Shimla: Himachal Pradesh Pollution Control Board.

52. **Pearce, D.W and Turner, R.K (1990)** *Economics of Natural Resources and the Environment*, London: Harvester Wheatsheaf.

53. **Pigon, AC (1920)** Economics of Welfare. London : Macmillan.

54. **Planning Department (2003)** Draft Tenth Plan. Shimla: Planning Department Himachal Pradesh.

55. **R&T (2003)** *Annual Administrative Report 2003*. Shimla: Railway and Traffic Wing H.P. Police.

56. **Rangnath, N (1995)** National Urban Transport Policy- a Framework. *Indian Journal of Transport Management, Vol.19, No. 2: 85-98.*

57. **Ravibabu, M (2006) Viability of Surface Rail for Urban Mass Transit.** *Economic and Political Weekly, April 22, 2006: 1506.*

58. **Reddy, C. M. (2000)** Vehicles Emissions: Beyond Technology. *Survey of the Environment, 2000.* New Delhi: The Hindu.

59. **Reddy, T.S, S. Gangopadhyay and P. Parida, (2000)** Planning for low cost transport modes in urban India, In Diaz Gonzaleg Palomas and Jamet edt. *Urban Transportation and Environment.* Balkema: Rotterdam.

60. **Roth, G.J. (1965)** *Paying For Parking.* London: Institute of Economic Affairs.

61. **S&T (2000)** *State of the Environment Report – Himachal Pradesh*, Department of Science and Technology, Government of Himachal Pradesh, Shimla.

62. **Schwab, C and C.N. Soguel (1995)** Contngent valuation. *Transport Safety and the value of life.* London: Kluwer Academic Publishers.

63. **Sibal, V. and Y. Sachdeva (2001)** Urban Transport Scenario in India and its Linkages with Energy and Environment. *Urban Transport Journal*, Vol. 2, No. 1: 34-55.

64. **Singh, R. (2004)** Economics of Judicial Decision-Making in India Tort Law, *Economic and Political Weekly*, June 2004: 2613-16.

65. **Small, K(1992)** *Urban Transport Economics.* Chur: Harwood Academic Publishers.

66. **Tietenberg, T (1995)** Design Lessons From Existing Air Pollution Control Systems: The

United States, S. Hanna and M. Munasinghe Edt. *Property Rights in a Social and Ecological Context: Case Studies and Design Applications.* Washington, D.C: The World Bank.

67. Tietenberg, T (1995) Design Lessons From Existing Air Pollution Control Systems: The United States, S. Hanna and M. Munasinghe Edt. *Property Rights in a social and Ecological Context: Case Studies and Design Applications*, The World Bank, Washington, D.C.

68. **Verhoef, E (1996)** The External costs of road transport in the Netherlands. *Blueprint 5:The True Cost of Road Transport. London: Earthscan.*

69. **Verhoef, E. T (1999)** Externalities, In Jeroen C. J.M. van den Bergh (edt) *Handbook of Environmental and Resource Economics*, Cheltenham: Edward Elgar.

70. **Whitelegg, J. (2003)** The State of World Transport. World Transport Policy and Practice, Vol. 9. No. 1: 4-5.

71. **Winston, C (2000)** Government failure in Urban Transportation, *Fiscal Studies*, **Vol. 21. No. 4: 403-426.**

72. **World Bank (1988)** *Urban Transport: A World Bank Policy Study*. Washington, D.C: The World Bank.

73. **World Bank (1993)** World Development Report: Investing in Health. Washington, D.C: The World Bank.

74. **World Bank (1996)** *Sustainable Transport: priorities for policy reform*. Washington DC: The World Bank.

75. **World Bank (2002)** *Strategic Environmental Assessment in World Bank Operations,* Washington D.C.: The World Bank

76. **World Health Organisation (2003)** *A Five Year WHO Strategy On Road Injury Prevention.* http://www.who.intviolence_ injury_prevention.

Index

L

M

N

O

P